THE FUTURE
OF AMERICAN POLITICAL PARTIES

The American Assembly, *Columbia University*

THE FUTURE
OF AMERICAN
POLITICAL PARTIES:
THE CHALLENGE
OF GOVERNANCE

Prentice-Hall, Inc., *Englewood Cliffs, New Jersey*
A SPECTRUM BOOK

Library of Congress Cataloging in Publication Data
Main entry under title:

The Future of American political parties.

   At head of title: The American Assembly, Columbia
University.
   "A Spectrum Book."
   Background papers prepared for a meeting convened by
the American Assembly at Arden House, Harriman, N.Y.,
Apr. 15-18, 1982.
   Includes index.
   1. Political parties—United States—Congresses.
I. Fleishman, Joel L.   II. American Assembly.
JK2261.F9 1982   324-273   82-13182
ISBN 0-13-345595-5
ISBN 0-13-345587-4 (pbk.)

Editorial/production supervision by Betty Neville
Cover design by Hal Siegel
Manufacturing buyer: Barbara A. Frick

10 9 8 7 6 5 4 3 2 1

ISBN 0-13-345595-5

ISBN 0-13-345587-4 {PBK.}

PRENTICE-HALL INTERNATIONAL, INC. (*London*)
PRENTICE-HALL OF AUSTRALIA PTY. LIMITED (*Sydney*)
PRENTICE-HALL OF CANADA, INC. (*Toronto*)
PRENTICE-HALL OF INDIA PRIVATE LIMITED (*New Delhi*)
PRENTICE-HALL OF JAPAN, INC. (*Tokyo*)
PRENTICE-HALL OF SOUTHEAST ASIA PTE. LTD. (*Singapore*)
WHITEHALL BOOKS LIMITED (*Wellington, New Zealand*)
EDITORA PRENTICE-HALL DO BRASIL LTDA. (*Rio de Janeiro*)

Table of Contents

Preface

Political parties are not provided for in the Constitution of the United States. Indeed, many of the Founding Fathers had an abiding aversion to the factionalism entailed in partisan politics. However, over the years, it became apparent that the efficient functioning of a federal system governed by an intricate pattern of checks and balances required the organizational assistance and discipline of partisan political parties.

In recent decades, there has been a sharp decline in the influence and effectiveness of political parties in the United States. In some measure, this has resulted from technological changes that have permitted political candidates to communicate with massive constituencies without the intermediation of the party mechanism. But, in larger scope, it has resulted from reform movements, which have been a reaction to the abuses of power and the corruption that invaded party organizations.

The result of these processes has been a breakdown in the political systems, as among the branches of the federal government and between the federal level and the state and local levels. Frustration resulting from this situation has caused many political leaders to propose fundamental changes in our constitutional system, with the risk of opening up the Constitution to incalculable consequences.

In order to address this problem and to examine ways in which the effectiveness of political parties, without their abuses, could be restored, The American Assembly convened a meeting among elected officials, political party professionals, academicians, businessmen, trade union representatives, and communicators at Arden House, Harriman, New York, from April 15 to 18, 1982. In preparation for that meeting, the Assembly retained Dr. Joel L. Fleishman, Vice Chancellor of Duke University, as editor and director of the undertaking. Under his editorial supervision, background papers on various aspects of the American political party system were prepared and read by the participants in the Arden House discussions.

Those background papers have been compiled into the present

volume, which is published as a stimulus to further thinking and discussion about this subject among informed and concerned citizens. We hope this book will serve to provoke a broader national consensus for a program to restore the vigor of our nation's political system.

Funding for this project was provided by The Rockefeller Foundation, The Atlantic Richfield Company, Arthur Young and Company, Mrs. Kathleen H. Mortimer, and Mr. David Packard. The opinions expressed in this volume are those of the individual authors and not necessarily those of the sponsors nor of The American Assembly, which does not take stands on the issues it presents for public discussion.

William H. Sullivan
President
The American Assembly

Acknowledgments

Acknowledgment is gratefully made to the following for permission to reprint excerpts from works published by them:

The New Republic for the excerpts from Michael Walzer, "Democracy vs. Elections: Primaries Have Ruined Our Politics," *The New Republic,* January 3/10, 1981, pp. 17 & 18. © 1981, The New Republic, Inc. Reprinted by permission.

W. W. Norton & Company, Inc. for the excerpts from Richard L. Rubin, *Press, Party, and the Presidency* and James David Barber, *The Pulse of Politics: Electing Presidents in a Media Age.*

Macmillan Publishing Co., Inc., for the lines from William Butler Yeats, "The Second Coming," from his *Collected Poems.* Copyright 1924 by Macmillan Publishing Co., Inc., renewed 1952 by Bertha Georgie Yeats. Reprinted with permission of Macmillan.

Praeger Publishers, Inc., for the excerpts from Jerald M. Pomper, editor, *Party Renewal in America: Theory and Practice.*

The American Enterprise Institute for permission to quote from *Choosing Presidential Candidates: How Good Is the New Way?*, pp. 7–8. © 1980, American Enterprise Institute for Public Policy Research.

THE FUTURE
OF AMERICAN POLITICAL PARTIES

Joel L. Fleishman

Introduction

In the disillusioning aftermath of World War I and the Russian Revolution, the poet W.B. Yeats voiced the now famous cry, "Things fall apart; the center cannot hold;/Mere anarchy is loosed upon the world . . ./The best lack all conviction, while the worst/Are full of passionate intensity. . . ." Yeats's words became emblematic of the fear among many of the best educated and intelligent individuals of his time that the twentieth century was destined to witness the destruction of the traditional bases of Western civilization. The apparent triumph of light over darkness in World War II led to a renaissance of confidence and even to lavish predictions about the beneficent future of "The American Century." Yet over the last two decades there has been a resurgence of the old fear that "the center cannot hold."

In the United States, one of the prime political reasons for this crisis of confidence has been the signs of disintegration in the

JOEL L. FLEISHMAN *is vice chancellor, director of the Institute of Policy Sciences and Public Affairs, chairman of the Department of Public Policy Studies, and professor of Law and Policy Studies at Duke University. Previously, Dr. Fleishman taught at Yale University and served as legal assistant to the governor of North Carolina. He holds advanced degrees in jurisprudence and in drama and is a member of the North Carolina Bar Association. The author of numerous books and articles on public policy, he has served with several professional and policy organizations at the state, regional, and national levels.*

traditional two-party system. As the power of the parties to organize and mediate the political demands of the populace appears
to crumble, a number of commentators have begun to worry that
a resulting "excess of democracy" threatens to turn the United
States into an ungovernable country. This sentiment has even
caused some eminences to call for far-reaching amendments to the
Constitution—such as a six-year, single presidential term or establishment of a parliamentary form of government—designed to
enhance the formal authority of political leadership.

While these chapters hardly scoff at the problems engendered
by major changes in contemporary American politics, none of
them yields to the temptation of exhibiting a *fin de siècle* fatalism
about the party system and the American tradition of democratic
politics. They recognize that the two-party system has itself contributed to the unhealthy condition of democratic politics. Yet
the chapters also display a number of convincing arguments that
the party system is not in a permanent spiral of decline but is
undergoing an admittedly painful transition to new political and
organizational forms of existence. Each of the authors has tried to
sketch the outlines of various proposals designed to smooth that
transition of the party system, as well as to revitalize its workings.
Although the prescriptions of the respective authors may differ
somewhat, it is fair to say that all the authors strive to adopt a
"realistic" outlook. As the always wise Reinhold Niebuhr once
remarked, realism should not be considered the monopoly of any
one distinctive viewpoint.

It would be misleading to say—as well as unfortunate if true—
that the chapters in this volume were concerned merely with the
party system as a self-contained mechanism. The introductory
essay by Gary Orren provides a general overview of the differing
models for the party system that have competed throughout American history as well as an assessment of the contemporary conflicts
over the functioning of the party system. The subsequent chapters
launch their analyses of and recommendations for the party system from specific vantage points, but all eschew a narrow or
highly specialized focus. James Sundquist examines the state of
the party system as manifested in Congress and suggests methods
for achieving more effective cooperation between the President
and the legislative branch. John Bibby and Robert Huckshorn
survey the party system from the often neglected perspective of

the various state organizations and offer encouraging evidence of their health. Chris Arterton analyzes how the present structure of campaign financing affects the shape of the party system, and, in turn, the postelection relationships between donors and office-holders. Finally, Pope McCorkle and I end the volume by discussing some of the ironies of the changing debate over the presidential nominating process.

We would be remiss if we did not acknowledge that this volume could not have been completed without the help of the many secretarial and research helpers at our home institutions. The editor especially thanks Cathy Ward for her rapid and accurate typing on this undertaking and many others, and Bernice Wheeler for managing the editor's schedule so as to permit him the space in which to complete this effort.

Gary R. Orren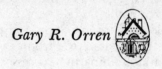

1

The Changing Styles
of American Party Politics

The modern political party is America's one innovation in representative governance. Other seemingly unique features of our political machinery were borrowed or adapted from the European experience, but the modern political party was invented here.

This innovation is all the more remarkable since political parties had to battle the personal prejudices of the Founding Fathers in order to establish themselves in the political life of the republic. Washington warned that parties were the "worst enemy" of popular government; Jefferson considered them "the last degradation of a free and moral agent"; for Madison they loomed as "dangerous" organizations that needed to be discouraged and controlled; and Monroe denounced them as "the curse of the country." Nevertheless, parties were created, in part due to the

GARY R. ORREN *is associate professor of public policy at the John F. Kennedy School of Government at Harvard University. He has served as a consultant for public opinion polling to the* New York Times *and to the* Washington Post. *Dr. Orren was a member of the Technical Advisory Committee of the Democratic Party Commission on Presidential Nominations (the Hunt commission), and he has written widely on aspects of this country's political system.*

grudging efforts of their original detractors, for one simple reason: they were indispensable.

In no other democracy has there been a greater need for an integrating mechanism like a political party. This need is rooted in two particular characteristics of American politics. First, America retains an archaic, eighteenth-century form of government in which power is fragmented within and among many institutions which share authority. The vast number of veto points in this system makes action difficult and inaction easy. Parties serve as a method for aggregating popular choices, tying these conflicts over courses of action to a broader program, and thus making compromise rather than veto the general form of resolution. Second, the demand for widespread popular participation emerged earlier and has proceeded further in the United States than elsewhere. The American public has achieved a greater voice in political affairs through the steady extension of the franchise, increases in the number of public officials subject to popular approval at the polls, and the involvement of citizens in the selection of party nominees. Political parties are needed to harness the participation of a powerful citizenry and fashion a coherent message out of the din of voices.

Yet at the same time, in no other democracy does the antiorganizational spirit run deeper. The ambivalence and even antagonism of Americans toward political parties grow out of our ethos of individualism. The suspicion of parties is one expression of the traditional antipathy to power and government and distaste for collective structures in general.

This conflict between the obvious need for political parties and the public discomfort with them (and recurrent assaults on them) is a continuing motif in American political history and a central theme of this chapter. Yet it is a theme that, in one of its manifestations, displays a particular irony. The development of mass-based political parties in the United States provided the key driving force behind the modern democratization of electoral power. Yet this democratization itself has actually diminished the strength, the vitality, and the stature of the political parties to which it owes its life.

The argument developed in this chapter proceeds in several steps. I begin by suggesting a typology of party competition which will illustrate the kinds of political parties that have dominated our history and which will reveal some of the principal arguments favoring and opposing each type of party. This will lead us to consider the forces that foster each type of party, especially the types of parties that are most prevalent today. My conclusions concerning the impact of contemporary parties on the capacity of leaders to govern will be disheartening, and will prompt us to assess some arguments for different types of political parties in the future. Such alternative parties, and the reforms that might encourage their development, will be the topic of the final section.

The Two Polarities

Our point of departure is with the two most fundamental polarities in our political system: the clash between ideological and coalitional politics, the division between strong and weak partisanship.

Throughout American history, academics and politicians have debated the virtues and limitations of the ideological and coalitional styles of party competition. The former involves offering clearly defined, often highly principled, alternative policies, usually based in divisive issues, designed to capture the allegiance of a particular part of the electorate regardless of the ultimate cost in overall support. The coalition style of party competition, on the other hand, represents an attempt to attract the maximum cross section of the electorate by appealing to all voters as potential supporters. This strategy uses noncontroversial, nondivisive issues which will appeal to the broadest range of voters without necessarily driving away any support at all. Note that what is referred to here is not the substance or direction of ideology, but rather the decision of whether or not to emphasize it and make it a central element in one's political arsenal. There are liberal and conservative ideologues, just as there are coalition-oriented politicians on both sides of the spectrum.

Almost by definition, these two impulses are locked in a perpetual tension. On the one hand, parties must stand for something. They must hold principles and present policy positions that are clearly different from those of the other party. Yet the parties must also come to grips with the simple facts of power in a democracy: they must win elections. And except in the very rare case where the majority of the electorate favors an extreme ideological position, winning elections requires compromise and encourages a party to appeal to the broadest range of voters from all segments of the electorate. At both extremes, then, is an alternative that is easy to reject: on the one hand, idealistic, highly committed parties that never win elections and, therefore, have no substantive effect on national policies; and on the other, parties that regularly win but have no principles and, therefore, no real conception of how to employ the power they have won at the polls. The key question, of course, is where to draw the line.

At any one time one of these styles is ordinarily dominant within a given party. History suggests, however, that this dominance exists only to be challenged. If the present balance favors the coalitional style, ideologically motivated constituencies (abolitionists, populists, prohibitionists, isolationists, segregationists, doves, hawks, antiabortionists) will inevitably pressure the party to take a more forthright stand on certain issues. They will claim —implicitly or explicitly—that their issue is too important, too fundamental, too "moral" to be compromised. On the other hand, these forces for ideological purity come up against an equally powerful urge—the desire to win—which pushes the party toward the center. A few serious losses will swing the balance of power back from the ideologues to the coalitionists.

An excellent example of these accordion-like swings is the history of the Republican party since the New Deal. Precisely because they are a minority party, Republicans have faced the ideology versus coalition dilemma with particular urgency. One group within the party has always asserted that in order to survive, the party needs to embrace many of the goals and principles of the New Deal and rest the party's appeal on its ability to better implement and administer New Deal programs. But such suggestions have always resulted in charges of "me-tooism" from the conservative ideologues. In their view, the Republican party is in a minority position precisely because it has refused to take a firm stand on the issues.

Thus, in the 1930s, the GOP stood in ideological defiance of the New Deal and received two crushing defeats in the elections of 1934 and 1936. As a result, by the late 1930s a new strand of moderate, coalitional Republicanism began to gain ascendancy. As best embodied in the two presidential nominations of Thomas E. Dewey, the moderates campaigned on the claim that they could deliver New Deal goals more effectively than the Democrats. The 1952 election was a clear showdown between these two styles:

Eisenhower, the moderate who used Dewey's rhetoric and support, versus Taft, the conscience conservative who attributed Dewey's defeat in 1948 to his failure to take positions different from those of Truman. When Richard Nixon gave signs in 1960 of continuing this coalitional style, it precipitated a minor revolt at the Republican convention and thus gave rise to the Goldwater movement in 1964. Even more than Taft, Goldwater called for a decisively, explicitly ideological party. His acceptance speech castigated moderation and embraced extremism. Unfortunately for Goldwater and the conservatives, their clear and coherent alternative received an equally clear and resounding rejection from the voters. The result, not surprisingly, was yet another swing, back to the coalition-style party, as embodied in Richard Nixon's candidacy in 1968. Following Nixon's repudiation in the Presidency, the Republican party in 1976 was split almost evenly between those who preferred an ideological nominee, Ronald Reagan, and those who preferred a more moderate, less ideological one, Gerald Ford. Ford, of course, ultimately received the nomination, but his defeat in the general election opened the way for the triumph of the ideologues in 1980. Deprived of their major claim to dominance, that they can win elections, those favoring a coalitional approach in the 1980 primaries were at a distinct disadvantage.

A second polarity in our electoral system is the clash between strong partisanship and weak (or even anti) partisanship. In a sense, this is the oldest issue in the American party system, since the republic was born in a climate of antipartisanship, and antipartisanship has been an important theme running throughout American political history. Madison warned that the first objective of republican government must be the search for the "methods of curing the mischiefs of faction." A century later, the Progressives advocated antipartisan principles and championed reforms to curb the power of the political parties of their day. Recent movements for party reform, particularly in the Democratic party, have advanced the ideals of antipartisanship. Even in the best times, Americans have been ambivalent and uneasy about political parties, treating them as "unavoidable evils."

As with the ideological-coalitional distinction, the partisanship polarity has nothing to do with the substance of a candidate's partisanship or partisan appeal. It is not a matter of Democrats versus Republicans. A strong partisan strategy stresses the symbols of party orthodoxy, actively seeks the support of party leaders, relies on the party apparatus to mobilize traditional party constituencies, focuses on partisan issues, and generally attempts to arouse sentiments of party allegiance.

Antipartisanship in this context refers not merely to the fact that parties have lost support but, more importantly, to the ways in which the party system itself may become the target of opposition. Antipartisanship threatens parties through insurgent movements and campaigns against politicians, incumbents, party regulars, and traditional party themes. This style is a prominent feature of recent party politics. Since 1952 most competitive presidential nomination battles have been won or seriously contested by at least one relatively weak partisan candidate: Eisenhower and Kefauver in 1952, Kennedy in 1960, Goldwater in 1964, McCarthy in 1968, McGovern in 1972, Carter and Reagan in 1976, and Anderson in 1980.

Four Types of Party Competition

Previous studies have drawn a useful distinction between two general political styles. They have called attention to the differing approaches of politicians who rely heavily on issue appeals ("purists" or "amateurs") and those who avoid or underplay such appeals ("professionals"). Amateurs or purists, according to this view, are portrayed as candidates who rely on what we have called an ideological *and* a weak partisan style, while professionals display more of a coalitional *and* partisan style.

However, the twofold distinction does not capture the full range of styles employed by politicians and parties. Take, for example, the battle for the Republican nomination in 1952. Robert Taft was clearly an ideological-style candidate, in the sense that the term is used here. He was an outspoken, highly principled conservative. However, at the same time, he was also a strong partisan professional—one, in fact, who was referred to as "Mr. Republican." His opponent for the nomination, Dwight Eisenhower, clearly was not an ideological candidate, nor was he a strong partisan. He made a very personalistic appeal, stressing coalitional and nonpartisan themes. Taft was both a purist and a professional; Eisenhower was neither.

Cases such as these suggest the utility of keeping the ideology versus coalition and strong versus weak partisan dimensions sepa-

rate so that we can identify four categories of party competition
(see Figure 1). These four categories are "ideal types" of party
competition since none exists in pure form. Each of the two underlying dimensions is unmistakably a continuous variable. That
is, parties are not simply strong *or* weak, ideological *or* coalitional.
Rather, they are more or less strong, and more or less ideological.
Since parties actually are situated at many points along the two
axes, we cannot identify perfectly "responsible" or "pragmatic"
ones. Instead, there are those that represent these ideal types to a
greater or lesser degree.

With this important qualification in mind, I shall refer to four
types of party competition. Each of these quadrants describes a
political history. It is important to note that each quadrant also
represents an argument about the best method for organizing
party politics. Each category has its advocates and opponents
among practicing politicians and academics. A candidate or party
style in the sense used here is not a mere idiosyncracy, but a claim
about how important party and ideology should be in defining
political issues and loyalties. Different styles do not coexist easily;
each makes a claim about the nature of politics which challenges
the claims of the other styles. The typology will serve as a convenient framework for summarizing the past and assessing the likely
future of American political parties.

Fig. 1.   Types of Party Competition

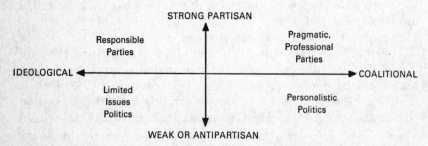

The Antiparty, Coalition Style: Personalistic Politics

During the colonial period and the first few decades of the
American republic, antiparty sentiment was nearly universal in
the United States. At this time, party government had but one
respectable philosophical defender—Edmund Burke. Political phi-

losophy before Burke unanimously condemned parties. The British republican tradition, which greatly influenced American political opinion, was especially hostile to parties, viewing them as a threat to traditional British liberties. Most of the American founders were determined to keep the spirit of party out of American politics. It is important to consider these attitudes at length, because they reappear throughout American political history.

The attitudes of eighteenth-century Americans toward parties can best be explained through a distinction employed by Alexis de Tocqueville. In *Democracy in America,* Tocqueville distinguishes between "great political parties" and "small parties":

> What I call great political parties are those more attached to principles than to consequences, to generalities rather than to particular cases, to ideas rather than to personalities. . . . On the other hand, small parties are generally without political faith. As they are not elevated and sustained by lofty purposes, the unselfishness of their character is openly displayed in all their actions. . . . Great parties convulse society; small ones agitate it; the former rend and the latter corrupt it; the first may sometimes save it by overthrowing it, but the second always creates unprofitable troubles.

According to Tocqueville and the Founding Fathers, great parties break society into hostile camps; they destroy peace and consensus. The example of the great religious parties, the Cavaliers and the Roundheads, was never far from the minds of early antipartisans. Just as great parties were considered intolerable, small parties were considered inexcusable. They created divisions where none had existed. They substituted narrow party loyalty for civic spirit.

Antiparty sentiment took at least three forms in the early decades of the republic. According to the first view, the United States had achieved a consensus on all important issues. This approach might be called Washington since George Washington himself personified this unity. Politics was to be carried on not by partisans but by experienced gentlemen and financial managers who took their bearings from the established consensus. While gentlemen might disagree about politics, differences of opinion need not divide them into hostile camps. Disagreements could best be solved through discussion tempered by congenial relations. Party organizations that tried to bring the electorate directly into such decision making would impede rational, dispassionate policy making and threaten to destroy social consensus. This version of antipartyism has been the most durable. In fact, several presidential campaigns in the nineteenth century invoked Washington's name to legitimate their own efforts to rise "above party."

The second antiparty position was Madison's. While Madison also believed that the great parties were dead—that the great principles of popular but limited government and the separation of church and state that had animated European political debates between the great parties had already been adopted in the U.S.— he did not expect all political controversy to die down. As his argument in *The Federalist* (No. 10 and No. 51) shows, he encouraged a multiplicity of factions, each competing for its own advantage, but each unable to win single-handedly. Factions would be tolerable as long as they were multiple. It was only parties that threatened to attract majority support that might become tyrannical at the same time. In particular, large inclusive parties could set rich against poor and destroy the advantages of pluralism.

The third antiparty view is that of Jefferson, the great party builder. Although Jefferson used party as a strategic organizational weapon, he never completely accepted party government or the idea that the alternating rule of political parties was legitimate. The Republican party was a temporary expedient required to bring the country back to its original principles. The fight between Republicans and Federalists could only end in the death of one of the two parties. Once the "great" Federalist party was dead, the Republican party could disband. The ordinary politics of gentlemanly discussion on the basis of social consensus—the Washingtonian politics described earlier—could continue.

The politicians of this era did, of course, create what has come to be known as the "first party system." This party system produced ideological partisans, but not believers in a party *system*. One of the major reasons for the decline of this party system was the continuing antiparty spirit of its participants. It was not until Van Buren's generation reached political age that attitudes toward parties and political styles changed.

As the franchise expanded, indirect elections dwindled, and deference to the gentry (especially the Virginia dynasty) lessened, it became more difficult for candidates to win elections without relying on partisan or ideological appeals. For better or worse, "personal" politics, at least as it could advance a career on the national level, seemed to disappear. But there have remained candidates who maintain that a political consensus does exist in the United States and that they personify that consensus. For these occasional "personal" politicians, the national consensus can best be attained not by partisans and ideologues, but by men of integrity and managerial and technical ability—men such as themselves.

Recently, the opportunities afforded this brand of politician have increased. Television permits direct, personal appeals to the electorate and creates "personalities" in a way newspapers never could. At the same time, the large increase in the number of primaries has made it necessary for candidates to build organizations loyal to themselves alone, not to the party. The decrease in the availability of party patronage has increased the importance of candidates' ability to attract a following based purely on personal loyalty. Whether this loyalty is based on charisma and sex appeal or an image of competence and integrity, it belongs to the candidate, not to the party or a policy program.

The Proparty, Coalitional Style: Pragmatic and Professional Parties

By the 1830s and 1840s, professional politicians were strongly entrenched in American politics. This "second generation" of leaders used party organization as a resource for combating the politics of deference and personal faction. In 1840 the Whigs showed without doubt that they were joining the Democrats in relying on party loyalty and extremely vague principles—in "going for the center," at least at the national level.

The party professionals who dominated nineteenth-century politics have been much described and much maligned. Foreign visitors Tocqueville and James Bryce treated them as the necessary evils of democratic government. Journalists and academicians, in turn, have shown disdain for their motives, their tactics, and their character. The party professionals themselves have been little concerned for defending themselves in theoretical terms. They saw parties purely as a device to build coalitions capable of winning the Presidency and other offices. Once parties had lost their stigma, the electoral success motive was sufficient to attract these professionals to a party. Not until the turn of the century did writers begin to fashion a justification for coalitional parties and their professional leaders. Lawrence Lowell and Henry Jones Ford, for example, defended American parties both against anti-party sentiment and against Anglophiles, led by Woodrow Wilson, who argued for the need for the "responsible" ideological parties discussed later. Lowell and Ford stressed the need for political parties to overcome the fragmentation of power caused by federalism and the separation of powers. But they warned that ideological parties could become class parties, pitting the wealthy against the poor and capitalism against socialism. Coalitional parties preserved the fragile American consensus, they argued, thereby protecting vulnerable individual rights.

Post–World War II political scientists have proven to be the group most willing to defend party professionals and pragmatic parties. The leading defender of the coalitional party and the professional politician was V.O. Key, Jr. According to his arguments —now political science staples—parties provide the right amount of choice for a society with multiple cross cleavages. Political alternatives do not come ready-made; parties must form them in order to give the electorate a choice and in order to have their choice make a difference. To give the electorate a real choice, both alternatives must be within the pale, that is, they must have a chance of being acceptable to a majority of voters. Parties thus must avoid issues which tend to fragment the electorate. But strongly ideological parties lack this necessary flexibility: they care little about the direction in which the majority is going, let alone about pursuing it.

According to this argument, the major choice the parties can offer is that between the "ins" and the "outs." Since power in the United States is fragmented, it is often hard to fix responsibility for public policy. Separating political actors into two distinct groups gives the "out" group the corporate identity and incentives to criticize the "ins." The "ins" are thus forced to take responsibility for and to defend their policies and programs. This competition focuses public debate and gives the electorate a chance to "throw the rascals out." Without strong parties, politics becomes a proliferation of issues and personalities. Candidates find few incentives for stressing their records or those of their opponents. Without parties, or with very weak ones, the tendency to avoid or confuse issues is even greater than with coalitional parties.

The rationale for parties that advocate compromise is itself a form of compromise. The supporters of coalitional parties want to offer voters *some* choice, but not *so much* choice that neither (1) agreement on basic principles would be destroyed and the country divided into hostile camps or (2) only one alternative, or even no alternative, would be considered acceptable or legitimate by the majority. Pragmatic, professional parties can be something more than Tocqueville's "small parties" but something less than his "great parties." Parties can divide the electorate so as to form a governing majority, but they can also provide the invaluable service of integrating new voters into the political mainstream. American parties may not win academic beauty contests, but they are the best we have—or can hope to have. Or so runs the argument of those who defend a type of party system which, ironically, is weakening just as its defenders become more respectable.

Strong Party, Ideological Style: The "Responsible" Party Ideal

Despite the apparent power of the party professionals in the nineteenth century and the increasing respectability of their parties, party professionals and their academic supporters have continually faced strong challenges from advocates of more ideological parties. This struggle has taken place on two fronts, one political and one scholarly.

On the political front, opposition to coalitional party politics has come primarily from the policy purists who want parties to present coherent and well-integrated programs, principles, and world views. It is safe to say that the United States has never had what the purists hope for, namely, two principled parties which offer the electorate a clear policy choice every four years. While the purists have occasionally gained control of a major party, their candidates usually lose (e.g., the Democrats in 1896, the Republicans in 1964, and the Democrats in 1972). The major exception to this pattern is the Republican victory in 1860, but, given the Civil War, this is not an example most purists relish.

The ideologically-oriented strong partisan, however, has been a consistent threat to the coalition-oriented professional, particularly at the state and local level and especially in the Whig and Republican parties. In the pre–Civil War period, a sizable number of Whigs—especially the group known as the "Conscience" or

"Woolly Head" Whigs—endorsed a strong partisan and ideological style of politics and objected to the pragmatic, coalitional ways of their Whig opponents, the "Cotton" or "Silver-Grey" Whigs. They also objected to the professionalism of the Democrats and asserted the need to bring morality back into politics. Similarly, during the 1870–96 period, the Republicans, especially in the Midwest, displayed a sympathy for strongly partisan, ideological parties. Richard Jensen has argued that the major difference between the Democrats and the Republicans in the Midwest during the second half of the nineteenth century was one of style. The strong party ideologues and their more professional opponents so hated each other that they mobilized virtual armies at each election. The Republican party, composed chiefly of members of pietistic sects, sought to bring their Christian morals into politics. Their major plank was prohibition. (The Prohibition party and the Women's Christian Temperance Union, as a result, often drained support away from the Republican party.) The Democrats, often members of liturgical churches, objected to this attempt at moral reform through legislation. They avoided the Republicans' crusading style until 1896, when Bryan stole the Republican's millenarian thunder, only to have McKinley defeat him through a return to a liturgical, pluralistic style. After the turn of the century the Progressives tried to revive the pietistic style in their battles with the bosses and machines, substituting for religious pietism a more secular, rationalistic, Protestant ethic. Their "reforms" eventually undermined the professionals' ability to keep their coalitions together. The reformers succeeded more in weakening all parties than in creating strong ideological, responsible ones.

While moralistic Whigs, pietistic Republicans, reformist Progressives, and their political progeny have devoted themselves to increasing the ideological purity of their own particular parties, only scholars have been sufficiently removed from party loyalties to argue for a system of opposing principled parties over a system of specific principles or programs. Woodrow Wilson was among the first American writers to hold up the British "responsible parties" as models for us. He argued that only unified, principled parties could accumulate the power fragmented by the Constitution, centralizing the government to the point where it could institute consistent policies. From Wilson to the American Political Science Association's (APSA) 1950 report "Toward a More Responsible Two-Party System," Liberals have had vague sympathy for responsible parties because such parties, unlike coalition ones, would bring centralization, direction, and thus "progress."

The clearest arguments for responsible, ideological parties have come from those who claim that the apparent consensus in American politics hides a real and serious divergence of interests between the haves and have-nots. According to this argument, first made popular by E.E. Schattschneider, nonideological parties maintain the status quo. Without principled party conflict, major issues—especially those involving redistribution of income—are never viewed as political issues. The have-nots are left out of politics because no party is willing to state a position which clearly has their interests in mind. Principled parties would put items of broad significance on the political agenda, increasing the electorate's awareness of truly significant social and economic problems and what is politically possible.

This view, as mentioned earlier, has had particular appeal to the left. But recently, as conservatives see the entrenchment of welfare state liberalism, they, too, have demanded "a choice, not an echo." Despite the appeal of this theme, ideologies have had great difficulty controlling the major political parties. Academic recommendations on responsible parties, such as the APSA report, have been greeted with deafening silence. One reason for this reaction has been that divisive issues do not separate the American electorate into two or three neat subdivisions. Ideologues have been hard pressed to articulate programs and principles which can unite a majority of voters.

Another reason for the failure of the responsible party model involves the loyalty of the ideologues themselves. Their loyalties are divided between principles and party. While the academician can value a principled party simply because it is principled, purists cling to a given party simply because it embodies *certain* principles. If their party loses an election, they are faced with the dilemma of deserting their principles or ruining their party's hope of recovery. Because they value certain policy goals so highly, they are also particularly vulnerable to splintering over theoretical niceties and to disputes over internal procedures. Thus, party loyalty often conflicts with their desire for ideological purity and their demands for internal democracy. This leads many ideologues to drop out of politics altogether and prompts others to turn to a weak or nonpartisan ideological style which we will here call "limited-issue politics."

The Antiparty Ideological Style: Limited-issue Politics

Major American political parties nominate candidates for a vast array of offices and claim to be capable of winning elections and convincing a majority of voters that their approach to governmental issues is practical and desirable. Ideologues may reject such parties for one or both of two reasons. First, they may believe that political issues are best treated individually instead of being lumped together in a package of party programs. This attitude usually stems from the perception that one issue overrides all the rest: slavery, civil rights, the Vietnam war, or abortion, for example. A second reason for deserting parties is the ideologues' despair of ever making them "principled." The ideologue who rejects parties for the latter reason does not necessarily reject the idea of party competition altogether. Principled parties may be possible once the ideologue, working outside the major parties, is able to awaken the "silent majority." Those who believe this can happen may campaign on the outskirts of established parties (as George Wallace and Eugene McCarthy have done). Or they may form third parties dedicated to revolutionizing the political consciousness of the electorate. Many of the pre–Civil War Whigs, for example, flirted with ideological third parties like the anti-Masonic party and the Liberty party. In either case, since they have no immediate hope of winning elections on their own, they are more akin to pressure groups trying to force regular parties to one side or another than to party members and loyalists.

In the United States, marginal parties which try to present a coherent world view have had little success. Ideological pressure groups marginally affiliated with parties have shown more strength. But the most successful ideological, nonpartisan groups have been those which have concentrated their attention on a narrow range of issues. Such associations, if they run candidates at all, usually run a limited slate, as well as a slate which does not claim to take responsibility for the overall governing of the country or state.

From Tocqueville's day to the present, America has always had a large number of such narrow-gauge organizations. Some have actually made significant inroads in electoral politics by stressing one major issue, e.g., the Abolitionists, the Prohibitionists, and the Dixiecrats. Limited-issue organizations are encouraged not just by the separation of powers and federalism, but by the Progressive reforms of the early 1900s and the more recent weakening of party organizations as well. The Progressives, following their town-meeting ideal, sought to increase direct participation at the expense of indirect representative government. The referenda they instituted proved particularly likely to stimulate single- or narrow-issue organizations. Moreover, the increased use of direct primaries has given single-issue organizations great leverage over the parties' nominating procedures, and television, in its turn, has given spokesmen for such organizations a vast audience. As parties' respectability decreases, the status and power of narrow-gauge "public interest" organizations increase.

Many theorists and academicians have praised voluntary associations and their effects on politics. But even supporters of pluralism like Tocqueville and Madison stopped short of suggesting that factions—especially those united by a passionately held opinion rather than by interest—should have direct or exclusive control over governmental policy. Most members of such organizations have been far more concerned with influencing particular policies than with justifying the limited-issue style of politics.

One observer who did defend this method of organizing politics was M.I. Ostrogorski. Since his remarks summarize the attitudes of antiparty ideologues, they are worth quoting at length:

> Does the solution to the problem of the corruption of parties not consist in discarding the use of permanent parties with power as their end, and in restoring and reserving to party its essential character as a combination of citizens formed specially for a particular political issue? . . . Party as a general contractor for the numerous and varied problems present and to come, awaiting solution, would give place to special organizations, limited to particular objects. . . . Party would constitute an association, the homogeneity of which would be ensured by its single aim. . . . Citizens who part company on one question would join forces on another.

This approach proceeds on the debatable assumptions that issues can be handled one at a time and that somehow the electorate will not have to elect representatives who must make deci-

sions on a wide variety of problems. Against the backdrop of
ordinary party politics and representative government, this style
continues to have broad appeal. However, its luster may dim as it
gradually destroys its major opponent and precursor, namely,
stable party loyalty and organization.

The Question of Consensus

The major disagreement among those four political styles
revolves around the basis and extent of consensus in the United
States. The advocates of personal politics usually maintain that a
solid consensus has been achieved and that governmental policies
can be developed on the basis of that consensus. Public-spirited
statesmen or technicians, if left unimpeded by artificial party distinctions, can advance the public interest. Often candidates who
emphasize this personalistic style use their own personality to
symbolize the nation's unanimity (e.g., Washington, Monroe,
Eisenhower, Carter).

The danger of this approach is that the supposed consensus
may be more fragile or shallow than expected. Even if no serious
cleavages exist within society, the public interest—the criteria used
to choose between competing policies and groups—may remain
obscure. Personal politics can degenerate into personal factionalism and unprincipled wrangling between branches of government,
as in the "Era of Good Feelings" or in southern politics as
described by V.O. Key, Jr. Presidents who rely on appeals to a
vague consensus may find that they cannot convince Congress of
the close nexus between this consensus and their suggested
policies.

The coalitional strong partisan, like the personalistic politician,
believes that the United States has achieved consensus on the
major issues of the day. No "great parties" remain. But those
who prefer pragmatic, professional parties deny that proper policies can easily be deduced from this consensus. Parties are needed
to present different slants on policy issues. Within the confines
of the achieved consensus, it is necessary to discover positions
which can receive majority support. To expect more than this, to
expect unanimity on all issues, is to ask too much of the nation's
consensus. Parties must aggregate interests to form a working
majority, but they should avoid stands which would destroy the
consensus already established.

The responsible party advocate claims that the consensus on which coalitional parties rest is illusory. Coalitional parties achieve consensus only by avoiding issues, especially by depoliticizing redistributive issues. Complacency, not disunity, is the greatest fear of the responsible party advocates. But they also deny that responsible parties need to divide the nation into hostile camps. Once a choice is made in a democratic manner, the opposition will remain loyal and will change its position to offer an alternative which has a chance to be accepted. Consensus can be achieved rationally through explicit choice; we need not rely on irrational tradition and avoidance of divisive issues to achieve consensus.

Antiparty ideologues also criticize the one-dimensional nature of American politics. But they clearly desire to establish a new consensus on some set of issues rather than to provide for a system of alternating principled parties. Actually, to single-issue candidates or organizations, the problem of reaching a consensus is hardly a problem at all. To some, it is solely the issue which is important; the principle involved is so important that any risk to unity is insignificant. On less volatile issues, single-issue activists see no threat to national unity from their actions and, more significantly, see no danger in fragmenting policy making.

Factors Influencing Political Style

While external political factors do not determine a party's or politician's style, the incentives for relying on personal, partisan, or ideological appeals will greatly affect their choice. Some environmental factors, especially the configuration of political issues which the party and candidate must confront, are in constant flux and can perhaps only be appreciated in retrospect. It is other factors—especially the constant decline in the loyalty of voters to political parties and in the resources available to party organizations—that are more predictable. Depending on their personal proclivities and their strategic predictions, politicians can react in several different ways to this continuing weakening of party.

While the factors encouraging the personalistic politics of the eighteenth century—deference, indirect elections, limited franchise, and lack of established national or state-wide associations—have disappeared, new forces are now working in the same direction. Personal appeals have partly filled the gap created by the decline in the efficacy of party appeals. The expansion of primaries has made it necessary to resort to nonpartisan appeals. Television has made it possible to make personal appeals to the electorate directly. Within a primary, the candidate who wants to "go for the middle" and thus avoid divisive, ideological issues must stress above all his integrity and technical competence. Stressing belief in an established national consensus will allow the candidate to win the support of weak partisans who vote in the primary and to gain the support of independents in the general election. Direct personal loyalties may also prove to be an effective substitute for political patronage which is no longer available to help build campaign organizations.

This style, however, has certain drawbacks. As the political arena becomes larger (e.g., as a presidential candidate moves from the early primaries to the fall campaign), the personal nature of the candidate's appeal will ring less true. Voters will be less certain of the candidate's integrity and competence as he becomes more remote. Moreover, fewer campaign workers will have personal contact with the candidate. As time wears on, the candidate must "routinize" his charisma. The personal-style candidate (especially the candidate of the majority party) who wins the nomination will have an obvious incentive to cash in on established party loyalties in the electorate and among other politicians. To gain election to office he must find a way to squeeze specific programs out of the vague consensus he put his faith in during the campaign. A President, in particular, will find it useful to give a partisan slant to the meaning of that consensus in order both to give his administration direction and to facilitate cooperation with Congress.

The key factor working for the coalitional strong partisan style of politics is the need of candidates—especially those running for President or governor—to find a method of organization for winning and maintaining majority support in the face of the heterogeneity and crosscutting cleavages of the electorate and despite the fact that most voters are moderate and nonideological. Party is a steady source of loyalty, supported by years of traditional affiliation. While issues and personalities come and go, parties remain. Personalistic and ideological candidates usually realize the benefits of affiliating themselves with parties, both for the sake of gaining control of organizational resources and for tapping traditional loyalties in the electorate.

As party loyalty and party organizations weaken, even dedicated partisans have had to develop new types of appeals. The use of nonparty issue appeals (what we have called a "limited-issue" style of politics) is obviously of importance in primaries. In local and congressional elections, where the voters can know the candidate personally, the personal appeal may be sufficient. But as districts get larger, ideological appeals become more useful. Ideological appeals allow a candidate to differentiate himself from his opponents, as well as to respond to the demands made by his opponents and key interest groups to "face the issues." Ideological appeals may be more effective in producing continuing loyalties, since the appeal of the charismatic, issue-avoiding candidate may last only as long as his appearance of invincibility.

The ideological, strong partisan politician must be able to reconcile his positions with his party's positions or, more often, his party's unwillingness to take positions. The ability of candidates to accomplish this is largely dependent on the nature of the issues dividing the political community. In particular geographic areas, taking stands on a number of divisive issues may help keep most members of the party within the fold and can strengthen allegiances as well as attract activists. But as noted above, this is seldom the case in American national politics. More often the marriage between ideological style and partisanship is an uneasy one, with each spouse trying to maintain an illicit life unbeknownst to the other. The partisan-ideologue must be especially adept at convincing the activists who form his organizational nucleus that he takes hard stands on the issues without alienating traditional party voters who oppose some of these stands. Ideological partisans who tip too far in the direction of pleasing party traditionalists in the electorate may find that they have lost activist support to other candidates or to single-issue organizations. Candidates who tip too far the other way may find that they have ideological supporters, but are no longer within the party fold.

Because of the inherent precariousness of the ideological-partisan style, the present weakness of party increases the size and strength of single-issue and fringe organizations. Such organizations allow the ideologue to retain his purity, even if his principles have been rejected by the electorate. Moreover, concentrating on a small number of issues can give the activist a greater sense of efficacy than can working within the mainstream of the party organization.

So we have seen that numerous forces are pulling parties and politicians toward a style of politics that relies on weak or antipartisan appeals, the bottom half of the diagram shown in Figure 1. Indeed contemporary politics seems to revolve in an orbit around this weak-partisan pole, passing in turn through two kinds of competition: an ideological style in which candidates such as George McGovern or George Wallace or groups such as environmentalists or antiabortionists make limited-issue appeals, and a coalitional style in which candidates such as Jimmy Carter make personal appeals to the voters.

If this type of politics—where voter choices are not guided so much by partisan cues as by issue appeals or candidate personality —has become the hallmark of recent American elections, we are left to wonder whether parties serve any valuable purpose and, if they do, whether they will again become an important part of our system.

Parties do, in fact, serve a number of very important functions, both during elections and in the governing process between elections. In elections, parties add an important element of clarity and accountability to our electoral choices. Compared to ephemeral candidate organizations or single-issue groups, parties have long, collective memories. They provide voters with reasonable expectations about how party candidates will behave in the future, and give voters a convenient way to pass judgment on past party records. Parties are potentially more important *after* a campaign than during it. The antipartisan, nonideological style which served Jimmy Carter so well in the 1976 campaign, especially in the primaries, proved ill-suited to the task of governing. His steadfast avoidance of any ideological categorization and his quest for a very broad, almost universal, coalition made his policy efforts seem "fuzzy" and provoked attack from both the right and the left. In addition, Carter's reluctance to discard his outsider image undermined the partisan loyalty and special interest support so vital to the success of his presidential initiatives.

Only political leaders with support in a party can hope to govern effectively. Where there is no sense of party loyalty or party discipline, political leaders find it difficult to get a legislative program through Congress. Our unique set of constitutional arrangements in the United States will only work effectively with the counterweight of political parties. Yet it remains to be seen just what *kind* of parties these may be. It is to this question that we now turn.

Toward a More Responsible Party System, Again?

The weak partisan limited-issue and personalistic politics of recent vintage are poor foundations for governing. To seek a sturdier foundation, we must look to the two remaining styles of party politics: strongly partisan-ideological "responsible parties" and strongly partisan but coalitional "pragmatic" parties.

Recently we have witnessed a revival of interest in more responsible-type parties. This newest yearning for more centralized, cohesive, and policy-oriented parties stems from two sources: the perception that it has become more difficult for the government to get its programs adopted and implemented, and the recent success of the Republican party in building the power of its national committee.

Political scientist Richard Rubin argues that political parties need to be recast into a mold that would help implement more cohesive public policy. "No longer have we the luxury of such abundant resources that we can avoid making hard policy decisions. Real choices—not just logrolling decisions (or no decisions at all)—must be made, and these will require not only stronger parties but also more policy-oriented parties than were necessary in the past." In this volume, James Sundquist argues that the medicine our ailing system requires is more ideological, issue-based parties. He sees promise for the development of such parties in the early signs of a possible ideological realignment at the elite and mass levels.

Christopher Arterton's essay points to the successful fund-raising and campaign efforts of the national Republican party as a harbinger of stronger, centralized parties. "Now the national committees are reaching out to help their state affiliates in a complete reversal of roles." He foresees the possibility of national parties acting like political action committees (PACs), distributing resources and services to candidates whose policy views they support. John Bibby and Robert Huckshorn call our attention to the nationalization of the Democratic party since 1968 through its reforms of delegate selection rules.

But the centralizing trend may hardly be so inevitable. In the first place, changes in communications technology may reverse the nationalizing thrust that characterized the early years of television. New technology—including cable television, video records, satellite-to-home broadcasting, and personal computers—may create a fragmented and decentralized style of communications (from broadcasting to "narrowcasting") and with it a more segmented style of campaigning.

Moreover, as Bibby and Huckshorn imply, the centralization of authority in the national Democratic party may have been more apparent than real. At the same time that the national party was consolidating its legal authority over state parties and the nominating process, a movement recently endorsed by the federal courts, the party was actually surrendering much of this power to the candidates. A number of the party's new delegate selection provisions yielded power to the candidates themselves and drained it away from the party and the convention. As for the recent resurgence of the national Republican party, it is not clear whether the growing organizational strength of the national party committee will yield greater control over candidate-centered elections, especially the nomination process. What is even less clear is whether the more centralized and powerful national apparatus will be able to enforce party discipline among Republican officeholders in Washington or the hinterlands. Some assume that Republicans in Congress will cooperate more with their leaders because the national party now wields a positive and negative sanction: the possibility of contributing or withholding valuable campaign resources (money, training, and technical services). While the influence of the national party may be crucial in a candidate's first election to the Senate or House, it is uncertain whether this will hold for incumbents. Incumbents will easily attract money from alternative sources (such as PACs) unless the ability of these sources to contribute funds is legally curtailed. In any event, the party will be reluctant to punish uncooperative members and thus threaten their own margins in Congress.

We *should* try to strengthen political parties, but this does not necessarily mean that we should strive to create parties which are more ideologically cohesive or more centralized, two key ingredients of responsible political parties. Both the feasibility and the desirability of that goal are questionable.

Forecasting the future of political parties requires a prophet's vision; finding lessons in the past is much easier. It has been no accident that ideological, coherent parties have typically died on the vine, and those factors that historically have inhibited their development are no less powerful today. The truth is that disciplined parties are doomed from the start: they run against the grain of America's institutional machinery and political culture.

The United States government makes a virtue out of protecting the status quo. Each step in the governing process requires bargaining, compromise, and negotiation. The need to construct coalitions of diverse interests and values undercuts the purity of coherent party ideology. For instance, in 1982 liberal Republican Senator Lowell Weicker, fresh from his vigorous filibustering attempt to thwart Senate antibusing legislation, received strong endorsements and campaign assistance from the conservative wing of his party in his bid to defeat ideological conservative Prescott Bush for the Republican senatorial nomination in Connecticut. Weicker's ideological opponents within his own party apparently concluded that despite his liberal views, Weicker stood a much better chance than Bush to win the November general election for the GOP and thus help retain the Republicans' tenuous hold on the Senate majority. This represents the triumph of pragmatic compromise over ideological purity that is an essential feature of American party politics.

One might hope that tinkering on the margins would transform our cumbersome institutional apparatus into a more streamlined engine for change. But no amount of tinkering will transform this apparatus from what it has been: the world's most successful shock absorber.

The nature of the electorate presents another barrier to the creation of more responsible political parties. Public opinion studies have consistently found that the American public does not think about politics in particularly ideological terms, especially as compared to citizens in other democratic nations. And to the extent that the public is ideological, its tenor is overwhelmingly moderate. Thus, it is hard to imagine a lasting division of the electorate into two camps around grand principles. It is equally hard to imagine sorting our national issues into two neat baskets.

In American elections, the most obvious issue to the voters, and the one they feel most qualified to pass judgment on, is typically whether a party or a candidate has done a good job or a bad job. They seem to understand instinctively that it does not pay to put much stock in the promises of candidates. Blueprints for the future are illusory: even if a candidate wins, the probability that he can actually translate his intentions into policy is remote.

The feasibility of establishing more ideologically coherent parties, then, is debatable; the greater question, however, is whether it is even a desirable goal.

As noted earlier, the most eloquent spokesman for responsible parties was E. E. Schattschneider. He favored a system with greater ideological coherence so that elections would serve, on the British model, as a choice between programs and policy mandates. His essay, *The Semi-Sovereign People,* is bitterly pessimistic about the prospects for American democracy in a system in which the major parties simply exclude a whole range of issues and fail to represent a vast segment of the population. People lose interest in the political process because it does not deal with the issues that matter most to them. Yet according to Schattschneider, real "oppositions" of political interest do exist in the United States, even if the political system is designed to exclude them.

V.O. Key, Jr., in *The Responsible Electorate,* defended the virtues of pragmatic parties with equal eloquence. He demonstrated how a system of competing party coalitions could allow for rationality *despite* the avoidance of clear-cut policy choice. In Key's system, the parties create coalitions out of each other's mistakes. Key argued that in order to be "real alternatives," both parties must be fundamentally acceptable to a majority of the electorate, i.e., "centrist" and "moderate." But what kind of choice does this represent? Key showed that in a presidential election, voters choose according to their evaluation of the performance of the incumbent administration. If their judgment is favorable (as it was in 1936), there is a massive shift of votes to reward the incumbent. But punishment can be equally swift and severe. The voters could hardly wait in 1968 to take back Lyndon Johnson's 1964 "mandate." Even though Johnson removed himself from the campaign and Humphrey tried to disassociate himself from his own party's record, and although no one could possibly tell what kind of alternatives Nixon was then proposing, the electorate behaved, in Key's terms, "responsibly." They "threw the rascals out" and put the opposition in. The Republican opposition was, in 1968, a *usable* opposition: it was sufficiently moderate to appeal to the centrist instincts of the American voters. Key noted that during the long dry spell from 1932 to 1952, many Republicans assumed that they were not winning votes because they were not presenting a "real" alternative to the Democrats. In fact, according to Key, the voters were afraid that the Republicans were presenting *too great* an alternative to the Democrats. A man like Alf Landon or Wendell Wilkie might try to undo the New Deal. The Republicans finally won in 1952 by nominating the moderate Eisenhower rather than the clearly conservative Taft.

"Real alternatives," to Key, meant that voters can actually choose between parties; that is, they can *switch* from one party to another according to their assessment of performance. If the parties are too far apart ideologically, if either candidate looks too extreme, then Key's system cannot work. Key's system requires alternatives which are both continuing—that is, partisan rather than factional—and moderate. In sum, he sought coalitions with a basic core of partisan continuity.

Key's argument, it seems to me, is more compatible with the institutional and attitudinal properties of the American political system than is Schattschneider's. The issues that work best in our system—and which, therefore, have dominated our presidential electoral history—are not ideological choices that chart the future but retrospective judgments of past performance.

Some political scientists have noted that after 1964, American voters began viewing the policy positions of the two major parties with much greater clarity. They concluded that if the parties offered clear-cut, well-defined policy alternatives, the electorate would respond ideologically. Political scientist Gerald Pomper, among others, cheered the possibility that the preconditions for a responsible party system were being established—a system in which "clear-headed" parties could stand as "groups of like-minded men." And indeed, the Republicans in 1964 and the Democrats in 1972 offered fairly well-defined policy alternatives, producing an ideological clarity which Pomper and others applauded. However, there is little evidence that the American electorate was particularly enthusiastic about the choices offered in

either year. It must be recalled, furthermore, that the parties offered clear-cut choices at a high cost—the cost of electoral suicide.

An additional problem with ideological parties is their propen-
sity to be dominated by single-issue or extremist groups. Historically, the American political system has always been characterized
by an extraordinary penchant for utopian moralism. Americans like to dramatize their politics as a morality play between
the forces of good and evil. Seymour Martin Lipset and others
have traced this penchant to our nation's Protestant origins
and the absence of a state church in America. But for whatever
reasons, our system is vulnerable to extremists on both the left
and the right (nativists, abolitionists, feminists, prohibitionists,
progressives, anticommunists, and the moral majority). Pragmatic,
professional political parties with their tendency toward coalition
and compromise are an important bulwark against moralistic and
extremist politics.

While people call for more ideologically coherent and distinct
political parties, along the British party model, it is instructive to
glance across the Atlantic to see what is happening in the mother-
land. British politicians and voters have been expressing deep
dissatisfaction with two parties they see as being too far apart
ideologically. The Social Democratic party (SDP), established
in 1981, has tried to stake out a centrist ideological position
between Margaret Thatcher's orthodox conservatism and the
left wing dominance of the Labor party. According to the original
statement of SDP principles, "Britain needs a reformed and liber-
ated political system without the pointless conflict, the dogma,
the violent lurches of policy and class antagonisms that the two
old parties have fostered."

Responsible parties are neither feasible nor particularly desirable in the United States. Yet they are sometimes offered as a
remedy for a political system sorely in need of strong parties.
Creating strong parties, however, is a different task from fashioning
ideological ones. Strong partisanship means that party leaders and
candidates emphasize party themes and symbols, that the endorsements and support of elected officials and professionals in the party
are sought and publicized, that campaigns rely on the organizational apparatus and networks of the party, that candidates stress
partisan issues, and that leaders exploit the allegiance of the
party faithful.

How then can we strengthen political parties, especially coalitional, pragmatic ones, in an age of rampant antipartisanship?

Recommendations

In a world in which political scientists disagree on almost everything, there is remarkable agreement among the political science profession on the proposition that the strength of American political parties has declined significantly over the past several decades. Regardless of how one measures partisanship—by personal party identification within the electorate, by party discipline in Congress, or by the vitality of party machinery—there is massive evidence attesting to the weakened condition of the parties in the United States.

The decline of political parties is undoubtedly a complex phenomenon, attributable to a wide variety of factors. Analytically, it is useful to distinguish three types of forces leading to party decomposition. In the first place, there are long-term social and demographic trends which have been operating for at least the last eighty years. The rising level of education, increased geographic mobility, and the growth of the welfare state have all made it substantially more difficult to maintain strong party structures.

On a second level, changes in the media, particularly the growth of television, have accelerated this long-term trend toward party atrophy. Television has promoted a personalistic and less partisan brand of politics. In addition, the media have assumed many of the functions once performed by the political party. The media are clearly a major force in the process of candidate recruitment, since they determine the personal attributes and qualities that a candidate needs to win. The media have also come to monopolize the old party task of evaluating and testing candidates—assessing how well they are doing and setting benchmarks for success and failure. Essentially, the media have supplanted political parties as the main connecting rods between candidates and voters, providing citizens with their only real information during the campaign.

Finally, the strength of American parties has been impaired by laws and rules, deliberately enacted by legislatures at all levels and by political parties themselves, designed to regulate elections, political parties, and the relationship between parties and government. Beginning in the Progressive era, the establishment of civil service merit systems and competitive bidding for government contracts deprived party organizations of most of the incentives they once used to reward party loyalists. Direct primaries similarly loosened the parties' hold over what had once been their chief source of power: the ability to grant or deny prospective candidates access to the ballot. Two major election reforms of the last decade have also influenced party fortunes: changes in the presidential nomination process and the passage of federal campaign finance laws.

Distinguishing among these three sources of party decomposition is important because it sharply clarifies what we can and cannot do to strengthen parties. The long-term social and demographic trends are almost certainly beyond our control. Similarly, for good or for ill, the growth of television is probably irreversible, and regulating it raises serious Constitutional questions.

If we are to strengthen political parties, we must exercise leverage where it is strongest, in the third category of factors—the rules and regulations governing elections. In particular, we should focus on the presidential nomination system and campaign finance laws, since both are of relatively recent origin and since there already exists some sentiment for modifying their provisions.

Having said this, it remains unclear how much effect we will have by changing certain election rules. It is a sentimental self-deception to believe that the amendment of election rules will suddenly revive strong party structures. Jeane Kirkpatrick has argued that "the most important sources of party decomposition are the decisions taken by persons attempting to reform the parties." I do not share that view. The decline of parties stems from a host of governmental, social, and political forces, and election reforms touch only one class of them.

Still, if we cannot reverse the forces favoring party decomposition, at least we can stop reinforcing them with election rules. More importantly, we can give political parties the necessary resources and flexibility to allow them to respond to changes in their environment.

Before examining the two recent election reforms, with an eye to suggesting changes, we should clarify the overall goals which will guide our assessment. Parties need to fulfill three central, and in some ways, incompatible goals. First, they must compete for votes in order to win. This objective involves the impulse to nominate candidates with wide appeal who can build broad-based coalitions and, thus, the coalitional style of politics. A second objective stems from the parties' need to oppose one another by offering alternative policy positions. The parties want to nominate candidates who represent the major points of view and interests within the party, which corresponds to the ideological style. A third goal of the parties is to nominate candidates who can govern effectively if they win. The parties are interested in having a nomination process that rewards candidates who are well-suited to the task of governing and discourages those who are not.

Parties then hope to nominate candidates who are electable, representative of party views, and able to govern. However, these three goals operate in conflict more often than in harmony. The competitive versus representative goals correspond to the coalitional versus ideological styles of politics, the horizontal axis in Figure 1. The governing function of parties depends largely on the vertical dimension in our scheme—the strong versus weak partisan styles of politics—since, as Sundquist notes, "The strength of the government rests on the strength of the governing party."

Our overall goal should be to restore a better balance among these three competing objectives. In the last dozen years we have witnessed a surge of democratic reform in American politics. Nearly all these reforms—loosening the tight grip of committee chairmen in Congress, eliminating fat cats from the financing of campaigns, and evicting the party bosses from smoke-filled rooms —were designed to enhance the representative goal of the parties but neglected their competitive and governing objectives.

To put the matter more mechanically, we need to make changes which will strengthen political parties and thereby move them up the vertical dimension in Figure 1, away from limited-issue and personalistic politics. At the same time, we must redress some of the recently created imbalances between the ideological and coalitional styles of politics in favor of the latter.

PARTY NOMINATION RULES

Since 1968, the rules controlling presidential nominations have been changed dramatically. Two basic purposes animated the party reforms: an effort to broaden the base of political participation in the presidential selection process, and an attempt to hold public officials, particularly presidential incumbents, more directly accountable by opening up access to divergent points of view.

To accomplish this democratization of the party, the Democrats adopted new delegate selection rules. These rules included: the substitution of proportional representation for "winner-take-all" as the principal method for allocating delegates, the creation of rules binding delegates to the candidates through the convention balloting, the phasing out of primaries open to voters registered in the opposition party, and the adoption of affirmative action goals for minorities and women.

These rule changes, together with encouragement from the media, helped to produce a doubling of the number of primaries (from seventeen in 1968 to thirty-four in 1980) and a doubling of the proportion of convention delegates selected in primaries (from about 40 percent in 1968 to more than 75 percent in 1980). In many respects, the sheer proliferation of primaries has had a greater effect on political parties than any particular new delegate selection rule. Primaries are not under the control of state and local party leaders, and the reforms made primaries the crux of the nomination process. Conventions simply ratify the verdict of the primaries. Before 1968 it was a risky strategy to pursue the presidential nomination by relying heavily on the primaries. As late as 1960, Hubert Humphrey could say, "You have to be crazy to go into a primary." No aspiring presidential candidate would agree with that today.

Unquestionably, these changes in primary and convention rules achieved some positive results. Before the reforms, some states employed secret caucuses, unpublicized procedures, and racial exclusions in their delegate selection; those were eliminated. The new reforms also genuinely increased popular interest and turnout in the presidential primaries, particularly in Democratic primaries and highly contested races. By way of contrast, state and local party organizations of the past usually preferred and often sought to keep voter turnout low in primaries.

However, the reforms have also weakened the traditional party structure. By vastly enhancing the role of ordinary citizens and stripping power from the party brokers, they enabled the media to become the critical link between the candidates and the voters. They tightened the grip that candidates exerted over convention delegates. They also tilted the primary process to favor outsider, long-shot candidates, thereby weakening the relative position of more established, better known candidates.

Spurred by these unfortunate by-products of rules reform, the 1980 Democratic Convention called for the creation of a Commission on Presidential Nominations, the Hunt commission, to review the entire delegate selection process, the fourth such body created by the Democrats since 1968. Even a participant in the commission can take issue with some of its proposals. As in previous efforts at electoral reform, the short-run political interests of key politicians and groups significantly shaped the commission's work. This is understandable—politicians live their lives in the short run, and it is foolish to expect them to design rules "for the ages." The 1984 election was never far from the minds of the rule makers.

However, from the perspective of *party building,* the intentions of the Hunt commission were unambiguous. The effort to strengthen the party was an explicit and implicit theme—perhaps *the* central theme—throughout its discussions, reports, and final proposals.

The commission's recommendations, adopted by the Democratic National Committee, aim to fortify political parties in several ways. First, they call for much greater participation by political professionals at the national convention. About 550 seats at the 1984 convention (representing approximately 14 percent of the convention delegates) will be reserved automatically for party and elected officials who will be permitted to attend without declaring their presidential preferences in advance. While preserving the influence of rank and file voters in the primaries, such a bloc of uncommitted delegates holds the potential for injecting professional judgment, peer review, flexibility, and deliberation into the convention. Other rule changes adopted by the party should create greater room to maneuver at the convention as well —for example, the relaxation of loyalty pledges which bind committed delegates to candidates and the elimination of the candidates' rights to replace disloyal delegates at the convention.

The "brokering" capacities of a group of uncommitted elected officials and party leaders remain uncertain: they might not act cohesively as a bloc and they might vote simply in lock step for the winner in lopsided contests and with their state delegations in close ones. Still, their mere presence at the convention could strengthen the role of political parties. Their involvement might keep the final outcome in greater doubt longer, helping to prevent the nomination from being decided very early in the primary season and enhancing the importance of later primaries. Most importantly, their involvement may encourage more discussion and perhaps even alliances between the candidates and elected officials. This relationship would help insure a more united national campaign, better prospects for the party in November, and closer ties between the legislative and executive branches. According to the new rules, House and Senate Democratic caucuses may name up to 60 percent of their members as unpledged delegates to the convention. Thus, a candidate may need to curry the support of congressional leaders to secure the nomination, support that would later prove valuable for governing.

The Hunt commission made several rule changes designed to enhance the role of state and local party leaders in the nomination process. State party chairpersons will attend the 1984 convention as automatic, unpledged delegates, and the state parties will select some 250 additional uncommitted delegates (with priority given to governors and mayors). The state parties also have been granted leeway to choose their method of delegate selection from among several alternatives.

Some of the Hunt commission's reforms do not directly benefit party leaders per se, but should serve to strengthen the coalitional goals of pragmatic parties. For example, two modifications in the system of proportional representation might give well-known candidates an increased edge over outsiders. Each state may adopt a "winner-take-more" system in which a bonus delegate is awarded to the winning candidate in each congressional district before the remaining delegates are apportioned by popular vote. In addition, states may once again establish "loophole" primaries in which individual delegates are elected directly by voters at the congressional district level. Such primaries can produce "winner-take-all" results for a candidate with broad appeal across a state, since a candidate can sweep all the delegates in a district with only a plurality of the votes. These modifications should diminish the value of "close second-place" or "strong third-place" finishes upon which lesser known candidates depend, especially early in the campaign, and should facilitate the building of consensus around a leading candidate. The commission also shortened the primary caucus season by five weeks. This might reduce somewhat the disproportionate impact of early contests in small states, and if so, this too will disadvantage lesser known candidates who generally thrive in such skirmishes.

So the Hunt commission did go some distance to redeem the place of political parties in the nomination process. Still, the final recommendations did not address some serious problems. Perhaps the most vexing problem is the growing number of primaries, which, as noted above, is probably more troublesome than any particular delegate selection rule. In fact, the proposal to modify proportional representation rules in primaries but not in caucuses might actually encourage more states to switch to primaries. A future goal must be to create a more balanced mix of primaries and caucuses.

CAMPAIGN FINANCE LAWS

In the 1970s, Congress enacted a series of laws designed to regulate how money is raised and spent in election campaigns. The effect of the finance laws on parties is somewhat ambiguous, since certain provisions benefit the parties and certain ones handicap them. Individuals may contribute more to parties than to candidates or to PACs, and parties are permitted to spend more in campaigns than either individuals or PACs. State and local parties may even engage in grass-roots activity without *any* spending limits. As a result, the law has redirected money to the parties and created some incentive, especially for presidential candidates, to raise funds for the party.

On the whole, however, the federalization of campaign finances has hampered political parties. Public funding of the presidential races goes directly to the candidates, further emancipating the candidates from their parties. The contribution and expenditure limits of the law have encouraged the use of media and direct mail. When the austerity of the spending limits or an inadequacy of funds due to low contribution limits forces candidates to cut back spending, they typically make those cuts in areas like local campaign activity and rallies—areas most susceptible to party influence and partisan flavor.

While the finance laws have hamstrung political parties, they have also encouraged the rise of other sources of funding and thus brought new competitors to the arena of election campaigns. The law has helped to foster the growth of PACs, which are the fastest growing source of money in congressional and senatorial campaigns. These committees directly compete with political parties for influence over public officials. Independent expenditure committees are another increasingly important source of competition for the parties. Unlike the parties, the amount of money they may spend is unrestricted.

The effect of the two prevalent styles of contemporary electoral politics—personalistic and limited-issue politics—are revealed clearly in the area of campaign fund raising. The raising and spending of campaign money is dominated by individual candidate organizations on the one hand and issue-oriented PACs and independent expenditure committees on the other. Neither relies on political parties and, in fact, both are often downright antagonistic to them. Thus, Congress has unwittingly rerouted money through less politically accountable channels than political parties.

If Congress were to retrace its steps and channel more money through political parties, it would face the question of whether to do this at the national or state level. Eliminating the spending ceiling on national parties in the general election would permit both parties to use the high visibility of the presidential campaign to raise substantial contributions. This change might strengthen the parties' fund-raising apparatus for nonpresidential years as well. It would also give the national committees enormous power over congressional candidates, which might strengthen the President's hand over an increasingly fragmented and recalcitrant Congress. However, given the exceptionally wide disparity between the fund-raising capacities of the two parties—in 1979–80 the Republican National Committee and the Republican House and Senate campaign committees raised a total of $111 million, while the Democrats raised a total of $19 million—such a proposal has very little chance of passing in Congress.

Political analyst Michael Malbin has argued that unlimited spending by the national party committees would have undesirable consequences. Giving the national committees the right to spend unlimited amounts of money undoubtedly would strengthen the already strong position of campaign technocrats. This would lead to greater expenditures on media advertising, rather than on personalized campaigning, especially given the pressures that the presidential candidates would bring to bear on the committees. Strengthening national committees while not attending to their state and local counterparts undoubtedly would mean that presidential politics and presidential candidates would dominate the parties.

Instead, Congress could extend the provision for unlimited spending by state and local parties for grass-roots activity, from presidential elections to campaigns for the Senate and the House. This idea would encounter less partisan opposition in the Congress and would create an incentive for the parties to use grass-roots volunteer networks every two years, rather than every four. It would strengthen the weak state and local parties and, most importantly, would promote a kind of face-to-face personal politics rare in our contemporary life, but without which parties will be hard-pressed to rekindle partisan allegiance. According to Malbin, "Rebuilding the parties as mass organizations and not simply as a central headquarters for technical services means making citizens care about them too."

Conclusion

Americans have debated the virtues and liabilities of the different styles of party politics for two centuries. Versions of each style have appeared, disappeared, and resurfaced throughout our history. At least since the days of Tocqueville, political scientists have mourned the decline of parties and predicted their demise. Yet the parties have survived both direct assaults and widespread mistrust, and even at their low points they have always displayed remarkable powers of recuperation. For parties did not appear on the original blueprints for this nation; the niche they occupy, they had to carve for themselves. And they have held their position through the vagaries of this country's worst political climates.

Now the spirit of weak partisan or antipartisan politics first contemplated by the Founding Fathers seems to have returned with a vengeance in the third century of this nation. The current oscillation between personalistic and limited-issue politics has severely impaired the art of governing. To begin with, these two styles of politics have given us a succession of unappealing leading candidates. Strongly partisan, coalitional candidates like

Hubert Humphrey, Henry Jackson, Edward Kennedy, and Howard Baker have found it difficult to succeed in the party nomination process. Weak partisan and ideological candidates have fared
much better: Barry Goldwater, George Wallace, George Mc-
Govern, and Jimmy Carter. Admittedly, these weak partisan
candidates displayed certain strengths. For example, they were
known for their honesty and forthrightness, and they exploited
this public perception in their campaigns. Some projected integrity
in highly personal terms, others in issue terms. In either case,
the voters generally regarded them as more candid and trustworthy than their election opponents. Of course honesty is a
desirable quality for public office, but other political and governing skills are crucial as well in our fragmented, divided government.
Among the final victors in the presidential race, the candidate
problem is even more acute: arguably, no two Presidents have
been less prepared in terms of prior experience in national
politics than our last two—Jimmy Carter and Ronald Reagan. Yet
inexperienced candidates are just what antipartisan politics begets.

Of course, no party style *guarantees* good leaders or bad ones.
The old system that gave us Abraham Lincoln and Franklin
Roosevelt gave us James Buchanan and Warren Harding as well.
Party styles and the election rules that support them cannot
assure the quality of candidates. But they do affect the way that
those candidates, once elected, will govern. If parties are not
intimately involved in our elections, then winning candidates, be
they good or bad, will ignore them once in office or treat them as
a minor annoyance. This will make the already difficult task of
governing impossible.

Over the last two decades, American governmental and political
institutions have become increasingly fragmented, atomized, and,
in a word, ungovernable. The decline of parties and the rise of
personalistic and limited-issue styles of politics lie at the heart of
this disheartening turn of events. Much of the fractionalization and
recalcitrance of Congress can be traced to the decline of party
discipline. It is the electoral connection that is the key here:
congressional candidates have come to rely less and less on party
ties and labels in their efforts to get elected and reelected. As a
result, they are more and more resistant to appeals for party
loyalty after they have taken office.

Things have not been much better in the bureaucracy, and again the decline of the political and partisan nature of administrative appointments is one of the chief culprits. Presidential appointments, at the cabinet and subcabinet levels, show a trend away from party politicians or spokesmen for interest-group allies of the President and a trend toward specialized policy experts and professionals. This depoliticization of the federal bureaucracy has weakened the control of the President over his appointees and made it more difficult to attract the support necessary to implement national programs.

Finally, the Presidency itself is plagued by party erosion. Presidential candidates run for office without relying on party organizations, by hiring media and campaign technicians, and by making personalistic and issue-oriented appeals to the voters. This approach has assured the growing separation between the President and his party. A President who must depend overwhelmingly on his personal image to sustain himself, who cannot count on the obligations of party elites to support him, is an isolated and vulnerable leader.

This is a grim diagnosis of the American political system. Many of the responses to this current predicament have been couched in terms of instrumental remedies, of modifications in campaign finance rules, primary procedures, or state party organizations. But all of these remedies only attend to the descriptive questions we have faced in our analysis of parties. They will work either to make a party stronger or weaker or to highlight policy differences between parties; they will not approach the important normative questions that have been a chief focus of this chapter.

To be merely in favor of party politics says too little. We must ask what kind of parties we ought to have and what kind of policy differences ought to separate them. I have maintained in this chapter that part of the solution to our current problem lies in the development of pragmatic, coalitional parties, for it is this sort of party that best fits this country's peculiar institutional and electoral constitution. This style of party politics, like all the others, reflects a particular vision of what party government in the United States ought to be and ought to provide. But it is precisely these visions that must be defended and vindicated before the business of party reform may proceed.

James L. Sundquist

2

Party Decay
and the Capacity to Govern

For good or ill, the distinguishing feature of the American
constitutional structure is the separation of powers. In their reaction against tyranny, the Founding Fathers deliberately designed
a system to forestall the concentration of too much power in the
hands of anybody—either a new King George III in republican
clothing or a legislative body too popular and egalitarian in its
make-up. So they scattered the powers of government—dividing
them between a national government and the states in the first
instance, then splitting the powers of the former among separate
executive, legislative, and judicial branches, and finally dividing
the legislative powers between a Senate and a House of Representatives elected independently of each other.

No one can doubt that this dispersion of power has served its
purpose well. Never has tyranny been a menace in the United

JAMES L. SUNDQUIST *is a senior fellow at the Brookings Institution. He has
held various positions in government service including deputy under secretary
of agriculture in 1963–65. Mr. Sundquist is editor of* International Review of
Administrative Services *and has served as treasurer of the American Political
Science Association. In addition to his numerous articles in the areas of
political parties and elections, national growth policy, and governmental
institutions, he has also written several books, the most recent of which is*
The Decline and Resurgence of Congress.

States. But protection against a threat from one direction has
meant exposure to danger from another, for powers that cannot be
assembled readily for the purposes of tyrants cannot easily be
brought together for the entirely worthy purposes of good men.
The checks and balances that have preserved the American system
have also proved capable of tying it into knots. The country is
vulnerable to a sometime inability of its government to act at
all, to the tendency of a disunified set of institutions to block one
another when there are pressing problems to be dealt with, and to
deadlock when there are crises to confront.

That is what gives to an instrument not mentioned in the
Constitution and feared by the founders—the political party—
its supreme importance. For, as V. O. Key, Jr. said many years ago,
"The obstruction of the constitutional mechanism must be overcome, and it is the party that casts a web, at times weak, at times
strong, over the dispersed organs of government and gives them a
semblance of unity." A Presidency, a Senate, and a House that are
divided by the Constitution can be united by a strong political
party.

The party is also the unifying force *within* each house of
Congress. The majority party in each house bears the responsibility for creating a functional organism out of a body of proud
and jealous equals, for organizing committees and assigning their
work, and for controlling the flow of business in committees and
on the floor. On the unity and cohesion of the congressional
parties depends the capacity of the Congress to enact with dispatch
the President's legislative program or, if it rejects his, prepare
and adopt an alternative program of its own.

In both these respects, then, the strength of government itself
rests on the strength of the governing party. And so the decay of
political parties in the United States, which has been going
on for a long time now but lately at a galloping pace, becomes
a topic of high importance.

The Prior Question: Is Strong Government Desirable?

Those who worry about the condition of our political parties
—and call conferences on the subject and write papers—usually
take for granted that strong government is good. Yet this is not
a doctrine that everyone accepts—not all of the time, anyway.

Like other democratic constitutions, written or unwritten, ours seeks to serve simultaneously two opposing virtues. On the one hand, the people—that is, the majority—should rule. On the other, the majority should be restrained from oppressing the minority. Most democratic systems, because most are parliamentary in form, are weighted toward the former of these virtues: all powers are vested in a legislative body, often a single house; parliament is supreme, checked only by its self-restraint. The American Constitution, in contrast, enshrines the latter virtue—the protection of minority rights, including the property rights that were much on the minds of the men who made up the Philadelphia convention. Hence the separation of powers, the checks and balances, the Bill of Rights, the innumerable points of veto were set up to protect the people against rash or impulsive governmental action.

To overcome "the obstruction of the constitutional mechanism," then, means to strengthen the ability of the majority to work its will. And in any period of history, there will be a minority that opposes the will of the majority and finds shelter and succor in the constitutional obstructions.

Throughout the modern period, it has been the conservatives who have opposed strong government, because the impetus for strengthening it has come from liberal activists who controlled the government and wanted to make it more effective for their purposes. The record of the conservatives on this score is totally consistent. They led the hue and cry over President Franklin Roosevelt's proposal in 1937 to "pack" a Supreme Court that was obstructing the executive and legislative branches, and at that same time they even made a constitutional issue of—and defeated —his reorganization plan to strengthen the President's control of the executive branch of which he is the elected head. Conservatives have consistently defended those devices created within Congress to protect minorities against majority rule, such as the Senate filibuster, the seniority system for selection of committee chairmen, and the obstructionist power of the House Rules Committee. And conservatives are the advocates of the long string of proposed constitutional amendments that would introduce new checks and balances to restrain governmental activism, most of them aimed at an activist Supreme Court, but some—such as the proposal to write a balanced budget into the Constitution—intended to prevent the majority from enacting policies the conservatives dislike. One might expect conservatives, then, to oppose on principle any move to strengthen political parties as the means for attaining stronger government. And, on occasion, they have sensed the connection and sought directly to prevent the strengthening of party institutions, as when they lashed out at the use of Democratic party caucuses to fashion and enact the legislative program of Woodrow Wilson's first two years. But most of the time the resistance to strong parties has been less direct, focused on limiting the power of party leaders—notably the President, but also the majority leaders of the House and Senate.

When conservatives are in power, of course, the shoe is on the other foot. Then it is their purposes that the constitutional mechanism obstructs. Yet conservative control of both the executive and legislative branches has been such a rarity—until 1981, only two years (1953–54) out of fifty—that conservatives have had good reason to fear strong government rather than to seek it. Even after the landslide election of 1980, conservative control of one of the power centers—the House—was highly undependable, resting on a tenuous coalition that the minority party had to put together without being able to use the House's institutional resources for the purpose.

Nevertheless, with the most activist conservative President in history in the White House, conservatives appeared on the verge of reversing their traditional position and rallying behind strong government. They hailed the unprecedented unity of the Republican party in 1981 when it passed President Reagan's economic program. And they sought to strengthen the web of party by electing a Republican-controlled House that, along with the Senate, would do the bidding of the President. Meanwhile, it was the liberals who found unwonted merit in the checks and balances. They pressed the Democratic House to obstruct and defeat the Republican party program. And in 1982 they were doing their utmost to strengthen the Democratic House majority in the hope—not expressed in those terms, of course—of deadlocking the government for the next two years.

Perhaps one cannot expect people to be disinterested when they appraise their country's constitutional structure. In any case, they are not. When institutional changes are proposed, most people turn automatically to examine the impact on their immediate interests. So they are for strong government when they approve of what they think strong government will do, for weakened government when they disapprove. They support a strong Presidency when *their* President is in the White House, a strong Congress to restrain the Presidency when the opposition holds that office. And the same with parties. Those who support measures to strengthen parties—when such measures can be identified—will be those who think *their* party will gain some advantage over the opposition or their faction will gain an advantage within the party or their party will function more effectively in their interests when it controls the government. Thus, conservatives today generally oppose limitations on what parties and candidates can collect and spend, while liberals are for weakening parties in general—but improving the *relative* strength of theirs—by supporting limits.

Given that institutional changes themselves are, like everything else, subject to the existing system of checks and balances, those who are unhappy with that system as such must find remedies that both the liberals and conservatives perceive as helpful to them. If strengthening political parties is to be a common objective, then both sides must answer the prior question in the affirmative; both must agree that strong government is good. Yet it may be that at this time both are closer to agreement on that fundamental proposition than ever before. Liberals have to acknowledge that the United States made significant advances toward the welfare state only in periods of strong government, and it will take strong government to sustain the advances. But conservatives must concede, also, that it required strong government to reverse the country's course in 1981, and it will take strong government to keep policies moving in that direction. As to economic policy, perhaps all sides will agree that the government has to have one. A coherent and consistent policy is likely to be better than an incoherent, inconsistent one, and, therefore, the government needs to have the capacity to make and execute a considered policy and set of programs. (Logically, of course, this suggests bringing the Federal Reserve System under government control, but presumably neither conservatives nor liberals would agree with that!) And what goes for economics surely goes double for foreign policy. In the face of international perils, surely the government needs the strength to act decisively in negotiating with allies and adversaries, making commitments, issuing and receiving ultimatums, and deploying military forces.

Nevertheless, if a unified government is capable of making and executing policy—whether in economics, diplomacy, welfare, or any other field—it will have the capacity to make mistakes. If it can be decisive and forceful, it can be rash and impulsive. So in the end, the question is one of judgment. Will a strong government make wise decisions most of the time? Does the greater risk lie in the capacity of strong government to carry out wrong policies or in the incapacity of weak government to establish any policy at all?

Those who find the former hazard greater have every reason to be happy with the current state of America's political parties. It is to the others—those who see a need to strengthen the capacity of government in order that it may act with decision and dispatch —that this chapter is addressed.

Causes and Consequences of Party Decline

When American political parties were strongest, in the latter decades of the nineteenth century, what held them together was not ideology or program—they had precious little of either—but patronage. Yet no cement is more binding than patronage, for making a living is at the center of everyone's concern. So the patronage-based organizations that were formed in wards, cities, and counties tended to be highly cohesive, whether tightly organized and boss-controlled in a Tammany Hall–type "machine" or more informally bound together in a rural courthouse clique. State parties, as federations of county organizations, were more loosely knit and factionalized, and the national parties even more so; but the party in power, at least, could use its state or national patronage to form a unified and cohesive organization on a broader geographic scale. So when the public finally revolted, in the Progressive era, against the corruption and waste associated with patronage and party machines at all levels, it struck at both the sustenance of the organizations and the machines themselves. The reformers succeeded in placing public jobs in civil service merit systems, in bringing favoritism in procurement and contracting gradually under control, and in enforcing the new laws not only through judicial processes but also through a new breed of investigative—then known as "muckraking"—journalists. And the reformers attacked the party organizations' fundamental power—the control of nominations—by inventing the direct primary, which caught the public fancy and spread rapidly. For a time, the existing machines were strong enough to dominate the new primary elections, but eventually, as their patronage declined, their hold on the voters slackened. Independent candidates who challenged the machines in the primaries turned out to have an increasing appeal, area by area, year by year. At the point, in each locality, where identification with the party organization came to be recognized as more of a handicap than a help, party leaders were compelled to withdraw from even trying to influence nominations. With little patronage to dispense, and without control over the selection of the officials who would dispense it, the old-style political machines decayed.

FROM PARTY REGULARITY TO INDIVIDUALISM

What took their place? Party organizations everywhere remained, in at least a technical sense, because certain ministerial duties in the nomination and election processes had to be performed. But in many localities the official party organizations did little else. Not only did they take no part in selecting party nominees, but they got out of the business of campaigning, leaving that to the nominees and their professional advertising agencies; and they might be disregarded in the distribution of the patronage that local, state, and national officials still had at their disposal. The political organizations that counted were personal ones, led by particular candidates or officeholders. And into the vacuum, also, moved the myriad single-issue groups that have grown in power and significance as the multiissue party organizations have declined.

In some places, however, the political reformers saw enough value in the formal party structure to seek to control it, and had the numbers to succeed. Then the vacuum left by the disintegration of the old-style machines was filled by a new and different kind of party organization. Its reason for being had to be, by definition, something other than jobs and contracts; it had to be what brought the reformers into politics in the first place—ideals and policies and programs. Those who rose to leadership in the new-style organizations had to trade not in patronage but in ideas, and they had to attract members and supporters by their ability to articulate a vision of where the city or county or state or nation should be going. In short, the new-style parties were ideological or programmatic—on the European model, although not consciously so. But they were also individualistic, for their leaders and members were, true to their origins, contemptuous of bossism in any form. The members and supporters resisted discipline, and leaders had no way of enforcing it, for they were not in politics to give or withhold material rewards.

Even when they might still be locked in a struggle for control with remnants of the old machine, the new-style politicians were often able to dominate the selection of candidates for Congress. There the machine politicians cared the least—how many jobs does a member of Congress hand out? And there the new, issue-oriented politicians cared the most, for foreign policy and military policy and economic policy are made by Congress. Frequently, a tacit trade was made: the reformers could pick members of the Congress if the regulars could choose the sewer commissioner. So the impact of the new politics was felt earliest, and perhaps most forcefully, in Congress. When enough of the new-style politicians arrived on Capitol Hill, the nature of the place was bound to change.

The new-style members of Congress, first of all, reflect the individualism of the organizations from which they come. The old machines sanctified regularity and enforced it, and those who came up through their ranks were accustomed to being regular. When they arrived in Congress, they were prepared to follow leadership and take their place in a hierarchical structure. They voted orthodoxly, predictably. But today's members are likely to have never followed any leaders at all from the beginnings of their political careers. The new-style members won their seats, in all probability, mainly by their own efforts. No party leaders handed them the nomination in the first place; they were self-selected, and they put together their own organizations, raised their own money, and ran their own campaigns. After they won nomination, the party organization may have helped, but in many states and districts—probably most of them by this time—candidates for Senate and House are largely on their own in the general election campaign as well. Such members are reared in self-reliance and self-sufficiency to survive and win in the absence of strong party organizations, and they expect to continue to rely on themselves after they are seated in Congress. Not having needed the party at home, and not beholden to it, they keep the party in Congress somewhat at a distance, too. The party leadership can influence them, all other things being equal, but it cannot control or command them. They have no habit of being deferential to the established and the powerful, and they are not that way in Congress, either in committee or on the floor.

DEMOCRACY, DIFFUSION, AND INDIVIDUALISM IN CONGRESS

Inevitably, ever since the first members spawned by antimachine politics began to arrive in Congress in the Progressive era, they have attacked the structures of autocracy built up in the age of the machine. Their first triumph came early, in the overthrow of "Czar" Cannon, the speaker of the House, in 1910—carried out, to be sure, in alliance with a good many machine politicians of the minority Democratic party. After that initial victory, however, the insurgents made little further progress in democratizing either the House or the Senate for nearly half a century, until in the late 1950s they suddenly acquired the critical mass of numbers that enabled them to dominate the majority party—by this time the Democrats—in both houses. Then the long-deferred revolution in congressional structure and practices could take place.

In the next two decades, the once inviolable seniority system was set aside. Several House committee chairmen were abruptly deposed, and that act at once guaranteed the sensitivity and responsiveness of their successors and all the other chairmen, in the Senate as well as the House. Committees and subcommittees were democratized, and the arbitrary powers of chairmen were curtailed. Power was dispersed to a greatly increased number of subcommittees. The House Rules Committee was effectively transformed from master to servant of the House. Party caucuses began to be used more frequently, though sporadically, to discuss issues of policy. In short, just as the tradition of bossism, or oligarchy, had been overthrown in the political parties of the constituencies, so was it toppled in Congress. And, as in the constituencies, the destruction of the autocratic congressional party machines has opened the way to the development of new-style party organizations there, participatory and democratic rather than bossed.

Yet, as in the localities, organizations of individualists are harder to form and to maintain. "No one can lead men and women who refuse to be led," David Broder wrote in the *Washington Post* in 1975 in diagnosing the ills of a "floundering" Congress. "The House juniors have overthrown the old power centers. Yet they consistently refuse to heed even those they installed in power." Four years later, Dennis Farney was echoing the same language in the *Wall Street Journal:* "It is . . . an atomized House, increasingly resistant to leadership." Speaker O'Neill found his followers "extremely difficult to coordinate," and Majority Leader Jim Wright and Majority Whip John Brademas expressed like sentiments. In the Senate, Majority Leader Mike Mansfield, during his long tenure, encouraged egalitarianism as a matter of principle. "I believe that every member ought to be equal in fact, no less than in theory" was his philosophy, and his successor, Robert Byrd, carried that tradition forward.

The leaders still have favors to bestow or to withhold, but they now rarely use their control of rewards and perquisites arbitrarily for purposes of discipline. Any leader who did so would flout the spirit of the times and cut short his leadership career. Cohesion in the new Congress has to derive, then, from the like-mindedness on policy and program issues of free and unbossed individualists. But the distinguishing characteristic of individualists is their aversion to subordinating their own views to anyone else's, and that renders the unity that now derives from ideology less solid and reliable than that which once was formed not alone by ideology but also by the sanctions once freely employed by speakers and by Senate oligarchs.

ARE REPUBLICANS DIFFERENT?

All these generalizations, it should be noted, are based on observation of just one of the two parties—the Democrats—for the Republicans have been the majority party in Congress for only four years in the half-century that came to a close in 1980. One may speculate whether Republicans will be different, if 1981 turns out to hail the beginning of a period of GOP ascendancy. Republican behavior at the outset of the Reagan administration was surely marked by an astounding degree of discipline—whenever the President took pains to attain it—but that discipline was imposed primarily from the White House rather than by the party organizations within Congress and, when the Democrats were in control, White House influence on legislators always rested tenuously on the President's standing in the public opinion polls.

The Republicans have, however, one combined inducement and sanction for building a strong, cohesive party in Congress that the Democrats have not had and can never expect to have to the same degree: money. The GOP has been collecting millions of dollars on a national scale and using those funds to recruit congressional candidates and to provide them with a substantial proportion of their campaign resources, including both cash and professional management services. The Republican candidates who win with this assistance arrive in Congress with what appears to be a deeper identification with the national party and sense of obligation to it than do the Democratic members helped less generously.

But once a new member takes his seat, whether money proves to be an instrument of continuing discipline will depend on the willingness of party leaders to withhold funds in future campaigns from members who defy the leadership. If past experience is a guide, it can be assumed that such penalties would be imposed only on the rarest of occasions, and the Republicans therefore, despite their greater resources, will encounter much the same degree of difficulty the Democrats have always faced in molding a cohesive majority party out of an assemblage of individualists. Except when they have a President who stands exceptionally high in public approval and who is willing to use his own tools of influence—appointments, projects, and so on—aggressively, as in 1981, the Republicans in Congress are likely to approach more closely the contemporary Democratic model of fragmentation and diffusion than the orderly, hierarchical pre–1910 pattern of the GOP.

A NEW NORM: DIVIDED GOVERNMENT

There remains one final consequence of party deterioration to mention. That is the unprecedented tendency, in the past thirty years, for the electorate to place one party in control of the executive branch and the other in charge of one or both houses of Congress. As party organizations have declined and voter attachments have weakened, voters have come to pick and choose on the basis of the varying appeal of individuals and split their tickets without misgiving—and the ballot reforms and antiparty doctrines that have prevailed since the Progressive era have encouraged them to do so. As a result, during the twenty-eight years from 1955 through 1982, the national government was divided most of the time, with Republican Presidents and Democratic legislative bodies—both houses being under Democratic control during six years of Dwight Eisenhower's incumbency and all eight years of Richard Nixon's and Gerald Ford's, and the House being Democratic for Ronald Reagan's first two years.

At such times, the normal tendency of the U.S. system toward deadlock becomes all but irresistible. The President and the congressional majorities are compelled to quarrel, for mutual opposition is the parties' reason for existence. Democratic majorities in Congress cannot approve a Republican President's program without raising his stature as a leader and increasing his prospects for defeating them in the next election. For the same reason, the President has to reject congressionally-initiated programs; he cannot concede wisdom and leadership to the opponents he is seeking to discredit and defeat.

In the later Nixon years and all of Ford's brief term, the divided government was virtually immobilized, as President and Congress denounced each other and engaged in petty and tiresome bickering over who was to blame for the ills that beset the country. When an aggressive Nixon pushed the powers of the Presidency to the limit (including some claimed powers, such as impoundment of appropriated funds, that the courts later held the President did not constitutionally possess), an infuriated Congress struck back, seizing its opportunities to put Nixon in his place. The quarreling branches made a hash of fiscal policy. Congress took command of foreign affairs, checkmating the President's policy in Southeast Asia and legislating an end to the Vietnam War. When Gerald Ford succeeded Nixon, Congress refused to acknowledge the secret commitments Nixon had made to President Thieu of South Vietnam and tried to set its own course in foreign affairs in defiance of the President and Secretary of State Kissinger— destroying Ford's trade agreement with the Soviet Union, casting its lot with Greece against Turkey in the Cyprus dispute, refusing to let the President intervene in Angola, and rejecting his proposed last-ditch aid to South Vietnam. Whether Congress's foreign policy was better or worse than the President's—and that will be endlessly debated—the fundamental fact was that in the absence of unity between the branches the country had no foreign policy at all. No one could speak for the United States. No one could negotiate effectively with foreign countries. No one could make commitments that would be respected. Meanwhile, in domestic affairs, the country was stalemated.

Under extraordinary circumstances, it is true, statesmen can sometimes rise above partisan differences. In the 1950s, President Eisenhower, a native Texan, managed to collaborate on foreign policy with the two Texans who led Congress—Speaker Sam Rayburn and Senate Majority Leader Lyndon Johnson—essentially because he sought only to carry on the policies established by his Democratic predecessors. But on domestic matters, the six years of divided government were years of unbroken stalemate and recrimination. In the first year of the Reagan administration, the President was able to pass his economic program because, with his fresh electoral mandate and firm public support, he would hold his own party virtually intact while exploiting the traditional liberal-conservative split within the Democratic party. But the Democrats still controlled the House's institutional machinery— its committees and subcommittees and the posts of leadership that manage the flow of business—and they could be expected to use that machinery to thwart the President and deadlock the government whenever they detected a decline in the President's standing among their constituents. Even before the first Reagan year ended, the partisan spirit appeared to be clearly rising among House Democrats while the cohesion of House Republicans began to fray. One could anticipate that the ills of divided government that frustrated Presidents Eisenhower, Nixon, and Ford would soon plague Ronald Reagan also.

Revitalizing the Web of Party

The destruction of the old-style political organizations, with their corruption and autocracy—has been the product of almost a century of continuous reform. Now, when modern-day reformers reverse the meaning of the word and propose to strengthen political parties instead of weaken them, what is it they have in mind? Surely, few would wish to turn back the calendar over all those decades and restore patronage-based machines and bosses, even if that were possible. The ethic that partisanship should not govern the distribution of public jobs and other benefits is surely here to stay, and so is the ideal of wide and equal participation by a multitude of citizens, led but not coerced by their leaders, in the affairs of parties. What reformers must look to, then, is the development and strengthening of the new-style political organizations that accept and are built upon these principles—the modern programmatic, ideological, issue-oriented parties.

Not much information has been assembled on what makes such organizations survive and prosper. The anatomy of the old-style machines has been dissected in minute detail by scholars, muckrakers, and novelists, but the reformed organizations are too new, too scattered and diverse, too changeable and even short-lived, and perhaps not colorful enough, to have attracted systematic and sustained attention. And while more is known about the ideological parties that are the norm in Europe, the differences in political milieu on the two sides of the Atlantic suggest that lessons from the Old World may have little relevance in the New. European parties operate within much smaller geographic confines, usually in unitary states; unlike the federated American parties; therefore, they have always been highly centralized, with authoritative central policy-making and candidate selection processes; they have had distinctive ideologies from the beginning, reflecting cleavages of class and religion deeper than any this country has known; and they exist, usually, not in a two-party but in a multiparty setting, which permits each party to cover a relatively narrow portion of the ideological spectrum and thus to maintain more easily its consistency and distinctiveness.

Despite these differences, a strong American party of the new style might well resemble its European more than its traditional American counterpart, because its strength would have to flow from the kind of ideological homogeneity with which European parties were born but which American parties have rarely attained. The last time any American party approached ideological unity was more than a century ago, when the Republican party was founded in a crusade against the extension of slavery, and the Democratic party responded by coalescing at the opposite pole. Once the slavery issue was resolved, both parties fell into feuding factions. The Republican party split between east and west, between financial and industrial interests and agrarians, and the Democrats divided on a fault line cleaving north from south, urban from rural, wet from dry.

So, even when party organizations in the localities reached their apogee of organization and discipline in the late nineteenth century, a federation of strong local bodies was not necessarily a strong *national* organization, and the party web was not necessarily resilient enough to tie together the President and the leadership of Congress. Governmental programs might be few, but Presidents and congressional barons could still feud over the staffing of post offices and customs houses. And President Cleveland and his congressional lieutenants could fall out over the tariff issue, President McKinley and Speaker Reed over the Spanish-American War, and President Theodore Roosevelt and Speaker Cannon over practically the whole range of public policy. Later, as the range of concern of government steadily expanded, the potential for disunity within the national parties grew proportionately.

Every four years, however, there is in the American system a powerful centripetal event—a presidential election. Each party must somehow forge enough unity out of its disparate elements to select a presidential candidate, and once he is chosen, the incentives to unite behind that candidate are considerable. For the winning party, the incentives to set aside differences are even greater after the election, for control of government must be organized and shared. Thus, for a period after each election, the winning party tends to coalesce behind its leader in the White House. The extent to which it succeeds in doing so depends, in essence, on the strength of the new President's mandate. If he wins office by a landslide, his party in Congress is likely to accept his leadership. How long it follows him depends first of all, as noted earlier, on how long he maintains his hold upon the country. Secondarily, it depends on his skill in dealing with Congress itself.

It is immediately after landslide elections, then, that the web of party is at its strongest. In such circumstances, the obstructions of the constitutional mechanism can be overcome and decisive new departures in public policy can be taken. The modern American government was created, for the most part, in three such periods. On each of those occasions, the Democratic party, as the party of governmental activism, was the instrument. Those three periods were the first two years of Woodrow Wilson's Presidency, 1913–14, when the measures that made up his New Freedom were enacted; the first term of Franklin Roosevelt, when the New Deal transformed American government; and, a generation later, the first year after the election of Lyndon Johnson, when the Great Society was written into law. And it was in another such period of party unity, after the landslide of 1980, that the Republicans were able decisively to reverse the course of all that Democratic history.

Such periods of party harmony, history tells us, do not last long. Wilson's New Freedom came to an end when war broke out in Europe and Democratic unity was shattered on the issue of preparedness; the New Deal Democratic party broke asunder on Roosevelt's plan to "pack" the Supreme Court; and the Great Society era ended when riots erupted in the cities and on the campuses and the party divided on Vietnam. In each case, the President lost his hold on Congress because he was clearly losing some of his support in the country at large. The web of party is a fragile thing; it will not be stronger in the government in Washington than it is in the constituencies of members of Congress.

THE PROMISE OF PARTY REALIGNMENT

Fortuitously, events over which the parties themselves have no control now bring the promise that the two major parties may shortly be—if they are not already—more ideologically united than they have been for more than a hundred years.

Each has had during most of this century, of course, an identifiable ideological cast. The notion that American parties "stand for nothing" and there is "not a dime's worth of difference between them," as George Wallace liked to say, has had little basis in fact since Cleveland's day. The Democratic party became distinctly progressive in spirit and program in 1896, when it first nominated William Jennings Bryan; it charted a wholly progressive course under the leadership of Woodrow Wilson; and, after losing its bearings for a time, it regained them under Franklin Roosevelt and maintained a course of reasonable ideological consistency through Truman, Kennedy, and Johnson. Jimmy Carter ran a campaign outside the party's twentieth-century tradition but returned part-way to it after his inauguration. In any case, most of the party's current leadership—despite its usual throes of introspection after a defeat—still fits the progressive mold.

The Republican party, in contrast, has had no serious flirtation with progressivism since Theodore Roosevelt. Once he was rejected in 1912—and left the party—its division has been only between the pragmatic conservatives, who recognized the political popularity of the welfare state and sought only to retard its growth and administer it better, and the die-hard conservatives, who denounced it altogether and tried—except for a few programs with the most intense and widespread support—to wipe it out.

The basis for ideological national parties, then, exists. The problem has been how to remake the state and local parties in the image of the national, when in the federated party structure each state—and to a great extent in practice, each local—party is autonomous. Within the Democratic federation, southern parties could nominate and elect Strom Thurmonds and James Eastlands to the Senate while northern parties were sending Hubert Humphreys and Paul Douglases to be their colleagues. When these worthies sat together, the very word "party" became a travesty. A President can represent the "mainstream" of his party, but he cannot expel from its ranks the legislators who wholly disagree with him, and neither can the party leaders in Congress—though, with some travail, rebels can be denied party perquisites such as committee chairmanships.

Yet now, not through any deliberate act of the parties themselves, the long-standing obstacle of the federal structure is being steadily diminished. The cause is the continuing realignment of the party system—the process set in motion during the New Deal years that has been working its way, ever since, through the party systems of the fifty states. Politicians and voters have been rearranging themselves on either side of the progressive-conservative line of cleavage that was defined so sharply in the 1930s, so that the diversity within each party is lessening year by year. In other words, conservatives in the South, or their children, have been moving in massive numbers from the Democratic to the Republican party while the shift of liberals in the North in the opposite direction is almost finished. Senator Thurmond dramatized the movement of conservative southerners in 1964 when he left the Democratic party for the GOP, and the election of conservative Republican senators from North Carolina, Florida, Georgia, and

Alabama in 1980—bringing the GOP share of southern senators to nearly half, ten of twenty-two—made clear how far the realignment had progressed. Earlier, in the North, enough liberal Republicans such as Mayor John V. Lindsay of New York City—or children of liberal Republicans—had become Democrats to enable that party to elect governors and senators in even the formerly most rock-ribbed of Republican states, like Vermont, Maine, and North and South Dakota.

As both parties have become more homogeneous across the country, their ideological cohesion has, predictably, been reflected in Congress. Because the realignment is most nearly complete in the North, the effects are most conspicuous in the Republican party, where today's "gypsy moths" appear as a nearly voiceless remnant of the once powerful agrarian and northeastern liberal wing of the GOP. The southern "boll weevils" are more numerous and more obstreperous than the gypsy moths, but they too are a shadow of the past, when southern conservatives and their allies made up close to half of the Democratic membership in both houses—and more than half of the key chairmanships—and thwarted Democratic Presidents and House and Senate leaders. The boll weevils will continue their decline with the continued progress of realignment in the South, and Democrats will be setting unaccustomed standards, too, of party unity. And, as the Republicans have demonstrated, the Democratic road between the White House and the Capitol will be less rocky, too.

STRENGTHENING PARTY LINKS BETWEEN THE BRANCHES

Every President since Franklin Roosevelt has made it his practice to meet regularly with the congressional leaders of his party when Congress is in session to discuss and decide on legislative strategy. Those meetings, usually held weekly, come as close as anything in the American system to institutionalizing the web of party, for the President holds the meetings in his house, sets the agenda, and leads the discussion not in any of his constitutional capacities but as party leader. It is his party role that makes the President chief legislator as well as chief executive.

Presidents and congressional leaders alike have testified to the immense value of these meetings. Crucial information is exchanged; the legislators learn in timely fashion the President's legislative purposes and priorities, and he in turn learns of the obstacles his program faces on Capitol Hill and its prospects for success. Together, the leaders settle upon their legislative priorities, the timing of House and Senate action, possible compromises and fall-back positions, and the rest. Subsequently, the leaders communicate the President's position to committee chairmen and other members and their priorities to the President, and all this lays a base for the artful and timely presidential telephone calls and invitations to the White House that are so influential on legislative outcomes.

Even when they subordinate their own inclinations to the President's, of course, the legislators retain their essential independence. Sam Rayburn liked to say that he had served *with* eight Presidents but *under* none. And so the accommodation of views and coordination of activity remain wholly voluntary with no means, when disagreements persist, of making decisions that would bind the party in both branches and thus unify the government (assuming the President's party controls the Congress). This has led over the years to many suggestions for the creation of more authoritative institutional devices for that purpose.

The celebrated Committee on Political Parties of the American Political Science Association, for one, proposed in 1950 a new party organ to unify not only the executive and legislative branches but all elements of the party at all levels—national, state, and local. Consisting of fifty members, including the President, Vice President (or, for the party out of office, its most recent nominees for those posts), senators, representatives, governors, and party officials chosen by the national convention, it would pronounce party policy between conventions, draft and interpret the party platform, and play an important role in candidate selection. It would be, in effect, the weekly White House meeting writ large. But the committee left most of the critical questions unanswered. How could a President be persuaded to share his power with a group outside the government? Why would congressional leaders wish to do so either? Even if the party convention required that they join such a council against their will, how could its decisions be enforced? The Democratic party did create, after its 1956 defeat, a Democratic Advisory Council patterned after the committee's proposal, but when John F. Kennedy was elected four years later he saw to it that the council was disbanded.

Others have suggested that the time to lay the groundwork for harmonious executive-legislative relationships is when the presidential candidate is chosen. If the nominee is someone acceptable to the congressional wing of the party from the outset, it is argued, he and the House and Senate leaders are more likely to work well together after the inauguration. Therefore, the congressional wing of the party should play a much larger role in the nominating process. If members of Congress and other party leaders had something approaching a veto over any prospective nominee, the argument continues, they could screen out not only candidates who would be difficult to work with but those—the advocates of the idea having just lived through Jimmy Carter—whom they could not accept as sufficiently experienced in foreign and military affairs, economic policy, and other matters with which the national government must deal.

When the party's membership in Congress made up the whole of the nominating body, as in the early years of the Republic, the screening mechanism certainly served those purposes. But it had another predictable consequence whose merits are debatable: during his first term, any President desirous of reelection found himself under the effective control of the congressional leaders on whom he had to depend for renomination; congressional "war hawks" dragged a reluctant President Madison into the War of 1812, historians tell us, by threatening to block his renomination unless he went along. No one is suggesting, however, that modern parties revert to any such degree of congressional dominance in the nominating process, and a somewhat larger role for party leaders and officeholders—such as the Democratic party's rules reform commission has been considering—would appear to add a useful safeguard to the process and to strengthen the cohesion of the executive and legislative branches without upsetting the balance between them.

Still another range of suggestions applies to the general election process. President Johnson proposed that members of the House of Representatives be elected for four-year terms, coincident with the President's. While he argued his case on other grounds, his motive was transparent: members of Congress who always ran on the President's ticket would be more likely to be his followers when in office. Some reformers have carried the Johnson scheme one step further, proposing to end ticket-splitting by requiring a party's candidates for President, representative, and senator to run together as an indivisible slate, just as the nominees for President and Vice President are bound together now. Such an arrangement would avert the deadlock of divided government most of the time, with the President's party always in control of at least the House (and the Senate, too, if the senatorial terms were shortened to four years). But even Johnson's limited proposal received no serious attention; much as the members would like to campaign less frequently, they instinctively rejected the scheme as bound to increase their dependence on the President. Why should members able to win on their personal merits—and incumbent members have all won somehow—tie their political futures to a presidential nominee whose identity and views they do not now know, whose help they probably will not need, and who may drag them to defeat?

Other proposals would amend the Constitution even more drastically, to unite the separated powers of the two branches. From time to time, reformers have suggested giving the President power to dissolve Congress and call for new elections, either with or without standing for election himself; giving a corresponding power to Congress to remove the President, subject to new elections; permitting (or requiring) the President to appoint members of Congress to his cabinet; or giving members of the cabinet seats in one or both houses. None of these ideas has ever acquired significant support, either by the elected officials themselves or by persons outside the government. The problem has not been perceived as severe enough nor the solution self-evidently suitable. Moreover, none of the proposed amendments can be seen as neutral. If a proposed change appears to elevate the President's authority at the expense of Congress—as in the case of the Johnson plan for a four-year term for House members—it is bound to be opposed by the legislators, and vice versa. Yet to succeed, any fundamental change in the institutional structure would have to have the backing of an overwhelming consensus in the country at large, which in turn would have to rest, surely, on full agreement between the President and the preponderance of both parties in Congress.

Short of constitutional change, the heads of the two branches could be required by legislation to pool their powers in some kind of joint policy-making body. The Joint Committee on the

Organization of Congress proposed in 1946 that majority policy committees be created in both houses and that these meet regularly with the President and his cabinet in a joint legislative-executive council—thus expanding the weekly White House meeting and giving it statutory sanction. The Senate agreed, but Speaker Rayburn rejected even the proposed policy committee within the House, and the idea has not been revived. In any case, it is not clear how a statute requiring the President and his party leaders in the Congress to meet together would be a significant improvement over the present arrangements. When the heads of the branches wish to meet, they may at any time—and do now. If they do not wish to get together, they would surely find ways to avoid holding even meetings required by law, or to turn them into essentially social gatherings where matters of import would not find a place on the agenda.

All of these proposals to temper the separation of powers through formal institutional change, whether by amending the Constitution or acting within its limits, have been wrecked on the same stubborn fact of political life: neither Presidents nor Congresses have ever seen any advantage to be gained by officially and permanently surrendering any iota of the cherished independence bestowed on them when the government was formed.

And it is difficult to see what could ever persuade them to do so. In emergencies, one or the other branch can yield, but on its own terms and with a short time limit—as legislators have delegated extraordinary powers to the President in wartime. But those are decisions taken freely. In crisis and normal times alike, freedom of decision offers to the statesman the greatest opportunity for benefit and the least risk.

So the links between the branches are likely to continue to be the web of party and nothing more.

HEIGHTENING PARTY COHESION WITHIN CONGRESS

While the cohesion of parties in Congress will always be limited by the extent of their ideological diversity in the country at large, party forms and practices within the two legislative houses still make a difference. They help to determine whether party members who are in fundamental policy and program agreement unite for effective group action or go their separate and individual ways.

From now on, it is clear, the forms and practices of congressional parties must be predicated on participation, equality, and democracy. Autocracy was shattered in the House in 1910 and died a natural death in the same era in the Senate, and the ancient concept of a hierarchy of leaders and followers—enforced by sanctions —is not going to be restored. If modern leaders are to forge strong parties, they will have to succeed in motivating an assortment of temperamental egalitarians to voluntarily submerge their personal interests, desires, and whims to the group consensus. This is a more difficult form of leadership, obviously—for it is harder to persuade than to command. More time has to be consumed in talk, more effort expended on opening lines of communication and keeping them open, and more skill employed in using them.

One central institution, clearly, is the caucus—the one place where all members of the party meet together. During most of their fifty years of dominance, the Democrats used the caucus scarcely at all, except to choose their leaders and perform the other formal tasks of organization. Once elected, the leaders found the caucus to be more of an embarrassment than a help. Lyndon Johnson as Senate leader saw no point in calling party meetings to hear the proponents and opponents of civil rights have at each other, and Speaker Rayburn felt fully able to set the party's course in consultation with a few chosen confidants, without submitting his judgments to a forum of the rank and file (or even a small party policy committee). Nevertheless, when Nixon and Ford were in the White House and the Democrats in Congress were under pressure to develop some partisan alternatives to the GOP initiatives, junior House Democrats won from Speaker John McCormack the concession of regular monthly meetings. The Vietnam War inevitably became the focus of discussion, and the antiwar firebrands had the preponderance of numbers if not seniority or influence. After a few sessions, the party elders who had supported the war began to yield to the pressure of the majority, and the caucus is credited with speeding the development and eventual solidification of a wide party consensus against continuation of the war. But after that, the caucus met less and less regularly. Often the conservatives and moderates denied it a quorum by finding other things to do. Speaker O'Neill, like Rayburn before him, came to regard it as more a nuisance than a tool of leadership and has rarely used it for his own purposes.

The Senate may have less need for the party caucus as a unifying instrument, for in that much smaller body informal contact and communication can cover much more of the necessary ground; a leader in the course of a week or so can talk directly with every member of his party if he needs to, and senators who need to resolve differences can readily be brought together in informal working groups. But in the House that becomes impossible, and it is difficult to visualize the development of a strong party organization without the caucus as a central agent. One day, perhaps, a politician whose roots are in a district that has a flourishing program-centered, participatory, new-style party organization will rise to the speakership and attempt to transplant its methods to the House. Surely then, he will make the caucus his own. And if he is determined to utilize it, if he sets a significant agenda for it, if he presides skillfully over its deliberations, if he makes imaginative use of caucus committees—as distinct from the bipartisan committees of the House—he may find it has a potential beyond anyone's current expectations. Perhaps it would not work; perhaps the ever-present, if muted, ideological divisions in the party would cripple it. Perhaps individualism has gone too far. But no one can be sure of the possibilities of the caucus until the experiment has been tried. After all, the caucus worked wondrously well the last time it was made the central mechanism of party government, even if that was long ago, in Woodrow Wilson's day.

Strong party organizations in the House and Senate, separately, would be only the initial step. If the houses go their separate ways, as on energy, welfare, and so many other matters in the Carter years, not much is gained. But to find a time when there was any significant direct linkage between the majority parties of the House and Senate, one has to go back in history even beyond Wilson, to the Reconstruction era. When the Radical Republicans seized control of reconstruction policy from the hapless President Andrew Johnson, their policy-making instrument was the Joint Committee of Fifteen on Reconstruction. Technically, the committee was bipartisan, but so few members of either house were Democrats—the southern states being still outside the union—that it was essentially a party organ. The committee guided the whole body of critical reconstruction legislation through both houses and to enactment over Johnson's vetoes. But since then, there have been no joint party organizations of any kind, and even joint bipartisan committees, such as the Joint Committee on Atomic Energy, have been rarities.

Nowadays, the links that exist between House and Senate parties are mainly those that pass through the triangular circuit that has the White House at its apex. If presidential leadership can coordinate all three elements involved in policy making, House-Senate relationships are subsumed—for the party that holds the Presidency. For the out-party, the problem of direct linkage between the two legislative bodies still remains, and in periods of divided government that gap in the institutional structure can at times be critical. Nevertheless, this is perhaps a problem that can wait. How to improve the internal cohesion of the parties within each house and to facilitate collaboration between the executive and legislative branches are the issues that demand priority attention.

Directions of Reform

The ills of the American political party system are deeply rooted in the traditions of political behavior in this country, entrenched public attitudes, and even the Constitution itself. The remedies will come—if they come at all—not through any sudden and sweeping reform measures but through the gradual development and adoption of new doctrine by the elite cadre of political activists and, through them, by the public at large, which will lead to incremental changes in institutions and behavior. With a sense of direction, those who would strengthen political parties can be alert to the opportunities that arise to shape those incremental changes and, in so doing, give birth and force to what may someday become a new set of dominant traditions.

In the preceding discussion, some of the ways in which the web of party can be strengthened within the structure of the national government were suggested, but it was recognized that the bonds among national officeholders of the same party are not likely to be more powerful than the party as a whole is homogeneous and cohesive on a national scale. So a set of approaches intended to improve the cohesion of the government in Washington must encompass the party structure outside as well as within that government. On that basis, my own list of directions in which reformers should try to nudge the party system include the following half dozen.

1. Strengthen the National Parties vis-à-vis the State Parties— Lack of cohesion within the governing party in Washington is

traceable in large measure to the fact that the national parties
have been federations of largely autonomous state organizations,
which are free to nominate candidates for the House and the
Senate who may be in total disagreement on major issues with
the national party as a whole. It is difficult to envision any system
whereby congressional nominees of American parties would have
to be approved by the national headquarters, as is commonly the
case with European parties. Yet in recent years, both the Democratic and Republican parties have established a greater degree
of control from the center, and this trend should be encouraged.
The Democrats' centralization has been expressed mainly through
rules governing the presidential selection process, the Republicans' principally through the use of substantial resources at the
disposal of the national party committees and private political
action committees whose policies the party leaders can influence.
The success of the Republican effort is perhaps evidenced, as
Huckshorn and Bibby suggest, in the remarkable degree of unity
of Republican senators and representatives behind President
Reagan's economic program in 1981.

2. *Strengthen the Party Organizations vis-à-vis Presidential
Candidates and Presidents*—Again the Republicans have shown
the way, in using resources not merely to promote the party's
candidates for President and Vice President but also to finance
institutional advertising for the party as a whole and financial
and technical assistance to candidates at all levels, down to and
including those running for state legislative seats. Since such
activity depends wholly on the availability of resources to the
national party headquarters—as distinct from resources in the
hands of candidates—a direct way to strengthen the national
parties would be to provide public funds to sustain party activities
between presidential campaigns. The same logic that justifies
the appropriation of public money to finance the campaigns themselves would appear to justify public support of other party
activity as well, but it would be subject to the same hazards of
discrimination against new and minor parties.

3. *Strengthen the Party Leaders vis-à-vis the Party Membership*—
This recommendation, in particular, runs against the grain of
the progressive tradition and the concept of democracy it embodies. Yet while in any democracy the electorate at large must
choose among party nominees in a general election, there is

nothing in democratic theory that requires it to make the judgment on the capacity for national leadership of candidates who
offer themselves in primary competition—and much to suggest
that that is a task for which the rank and file of voters is ill-
equipped. Before the vast proliferation of primaries in the
1970s, the presidential selection system had an admirable balance.
The relatively few primaries enabled candidates to demonstrate
their popular appeal, but the national political leadership—
senators, representatives, governors, mayors, and other party
leaders—could exercise a peer review and, when necessary, a veto.
That balance needs to be restored. Reduction in the number of
primaries should be encouraged, but even if that occurs, the
caucuses that take their place will be—and should be—open to the
widest possible participation. The solution therefore appears to
lie in the reservation of a proportion of convention seats for uncommitted officeholders and party leaders, along the lines of the
proposal the Hunt commission has advanced for the Democratic
party. What the right balance may be will have to be worked
out through experimentation, but one provocative suggestion is
for a bicameral nominating convention, with a nominee having
to win the support of *both* the popularly chosen element in the
convention and the element made up of *ex officio* officeholders
and party leaders.

*4. Strengthen the Party Bonds between the Legislative and
Executive Branches*—Proposals for new institutional devices for
this purpose appear impracticable for reasons discussed earlier.
But the informal relationships that have evolved instead depend
for their success on a sense of collective party responsibility among
those participating. Presidents have to admit the congressional
party into genuine participation in policy formulation—as distinct
from pronouncing party policy on their own and then attributing
narrow, parochial, or corrupt motives to members of Congress
who disagree. Presidents have to refrain from unilateral announce-
ments of legislative strategy, priorities, and timing from the White
House. In return, congressional leaders have to see to it that the
committee chairmen to whom legislative action on presidential
proposals is entrusted are not in fact narrow, parochial, corrupt,
or otherwise unresponsive to the will of the party as a whole. This
leads directly to the next suggestion.

5. Strengthen the Party Apparatus within the Congress—This means the development of the influence of the party leadership, the party policy and steering committees, and particularly the party caucuses, as discussed earlier. The caucus should become steadily more assertive in informing committee chairmen and members of the will of the party membership and relieving of their committee assignments those who are unresponsive to it. This would require great innovative skill on the part of the speaker of the House—and, in the Senate, the majority leader—especially in creating and utilizing a structure of party committees to develop policy positions that the caucus could endorse. Such a procedure would add new complications to an already cumbersome and overloaded legislative process, but there are promising precedents for its use. In any case, it appears to be the route toward obtaining cohesion and order in a Congress that has become fragmented and—except insofar as it abdicates to presidential dictate—anarchical.

6. Discourage the Split-ticket Voting that Leads to Divided Government—Any measures that strengthen the unity and homogeneity of the national parties, as suggested in the first three points, will tend to discourage split-ticket voting. But the evils of divided government are so severe that creative thinking is needed to devise other measures also. Constitutional amendment to require voters to vote for party slates of candidates for President, Vice President, and House (and perhaps Senate also) is one effective solution, though hardly a feasible one in the short run. Short of amending the Constitution, much can be done through modifying election laws and the design of ballots and voting machine layouts to discourage rather than encourage split-ticket voting for national offices.

For all these purposes, the first requirement is to recognize the profound truth in Key's metaphor: the party truly *is* the web.

Robert J. Huckshorn and John F. Bibby

3

State Parties
in an Era of Political Change

The nature and extent of leadership a President and other national leaders may exercise are significantly affected by the personality, political acumen, and skills of the incumbents. But leadership does not occur in a vacuum. It is both facilitated and limited by contextual factors—the tenor of the times (e.g., the existence of international and domestic crises), divided partisan control of the White House and Congress, the size of party majorities in one or both houses of Congress, the extent of party unity, partisan divisions in the electorate, public attitudes on major issues of public policy, and the capacity of political institutions to reconcile the inherent conflicts within American society.

Formerly chairman of the Department of Political Science, ROBERT J. HUCK-SHORN is now dean of the College of Social Science at Florida Atlantic University. Dr. Huckshorn has written numerous articles and papers on politics. He is the author of Political Parties in America and Party Leadership in the States.

JOHN F. BIBBY is professor of political science and former chairman of the department at the University of Wisconsin–Milwaukee. An adjunct scholar of the American Enterprise Institute in Washington, D.C., Dr. Bibby has also written books and numerous articles on various aspects of the U.S. political system.

Because so many of these contextual variables have partisan dimensions, it is clear that political parties play a critical role in shaping the environment within which leadership can occur. Parties also affect the leadership equation through their role in the recruitment, nomination, and election of public officials. So pervasive has been the influence of parties that in 1942 political scientist E. E. Schattschneider opened his classic treatise with the statement that parties "have played a major role as the makers of government . . . political parties created democracy and . . . modern democracy is unthinkable save in terms of parties." Schattschneider's assertion of the indispensable quality of parties reflects the fact that in those nations which have succeeded in holding free elections on a continuing basis, political parties are an integral part of both the electoral and governance processes. Indeed, the development of parties in the western democracies was closely related to the extension of the suffrage and the need for institutions that could organize the vote. Parties have also played a critical role in organizing governments, both in parliamentary and presidential regimes, and in helping mobilize the coalitions within government and the public which permit effective governance.

More recently, the *Washington Post*'s astute political columnist David Broder captured the centrality and essential nature of the American parties when he noted that there has to be

> . . . some institution that will sort out, weigh, and to the extent possible, reconcile the myriad conflicting needs and demands of individuals, groups, interests, communities and regions in this diverse continental republic; organize them for the contest for public office; and then serve as a link between constituencies and the men chosen to govern.

Because the political parties have been so widely viewed as the principal intermediary institution between the people and their government, as well as the primary mechanism for organizing governments, any change in the parties is likely to have far reaching consequences for governance. In this chapter, therefore, we present an account of twentieth century changes that have affected the American party system, while paying special attention to a series of major trends that have been operative since the early 1960s. Our analysis of these trends focuses upon the impact that the changes have had on the state parties. The reason for this focus is the traditionally prominent place accorded to the state parties by students of American politics. In the decentralized party system that has prevailed, the state parties have enjoyed substantial independence from national organizational control. In fact, the late political scientist V.O. Key, Jr. concluded that the American party structure is more nearly confederate than it is federal in nature. Therefore, when considering the American party system, it is essential not just to think of the two national parties, but to remember that there are also one hundred different party organizations in the fifty states. They, too, have an important role in helping to shape national political institutions. To set the stage for our discussion of recent changes in the relationship between the national and state parties, we will briefly review the party system as it existed prior to the early 1960s.

Changes in the Pre–1960s Political Party System

The Founding Fathers, who contrived an imaginative, intricate, and interlocking structure of national and state governments, feared political parties and failed to provide for them in their scheme of politics. In spite of this omission, the need for parties for electioneering and governing purposes quickly became apparent, so that by the 1830s party organizations were relatively well developed in many areas of the nation. From the Civil War into the early years of this century, party organizations held a near monopoly over the key resources of politics. Candidates were recruited and nominated through party channels giving party officials a dominant voice in determining who would carry the party flag in elections. Campaign resources were largely under party control. Precinct lists, upon which canvassing and "get-out-the-vote" drives were based, were the responsibility of local party leaders. The funding of campaigns was largely in the hands of party leaders, who not only raised the money, but distributed it to favored candidates. Thousands of government jobs were available and were used by party leaders as political currency with which to reward the faithful. Thus, the strength of American parties was grounded in the legal and practical monopolies they held over the three resources necessary to party success: legitimacy, nominations, and campaign resources.

The legitimacy of parties was manifest in the longstanding loyalty of their supporters. Most citizens were born into a party, retained their party identification throughout their lives, and tended to vote a straight party ticket. Political recruitment and nomination were dominated by the party organizations, and party leaders often could control entry into the political arena as well as promotion to higher office. The distribution of campaign resources was largely controlled by party leaders, enabling them to exercise influence over those who ran for office under the party's banner. Even with these strong parties, the American party system never approached the "responsible party" model, but they did occupy an influential niche in the political order.

American parties were the principal institutional casualties of the Progressive reform era which followed the Spanish-American War and extended into the 1920s. Progressive reformers, led by such persons as Robert M. LaFollette of Wisconsin, succeeded in securing adoption by many state legislatures of a series of institutional innovations designed to bring government closer to the people. While progressive reforms were intended to strengthen democracy, one of their major consequences was an undercutting of the role of parties. Candidate and interest group appeals directly to the public, without the party acting as an intermediary, were possible through the direct primary system of nominations, direct election of United States senators, initiative and referendum, and the presidential primary.

At the local level other party-weakening reforms brought the city manager system to many small- and medium-sized communities and replaced partisan-elected local officials with professionally trained nonpartisan administrators who would presumably be above politics. This development was usually accompanied by the imposition of a civil service system based upon the merit system, which effectively removed patronage from the arsenal of political weapons available to local party leaders. Furthermore, under the new reforms, many elected local leaders were subject to recall from office. The point here is not that these innovations were bad; indeed, most of them have been widely accepted by the public. Regardless of whether or not they have enhanced democracy, their overall effect has been to bring about a considerable weakening of the political party system.

It should be noted, too, that party leaders themselves sometimes contributed to the growth in popular support for the Progressive reforms. Widespread political corruption, often perpetrated by party leaders or in connivance with them, had undermined public trust in the parties. This was not only the era of reform; it was also the era of political bosses and machine politics.

Later in the 1930s, Franklin Roosevelt's New Deal helped to further undermine the parties by assuming their traditional social welfare functions. Party organizations ceased to be the providers of welfare benefits as an elaborate social service bureaucracy staffed by civil servants emerged. Recipients of these governmentally provided services were no longer required to pass a test of partisan loyalty, a serious blow to the prestige and responsibility of the state and local party leader.

Post–1960s Changes in the Political Party System

Since the early 1960s a series of changes has taken place in the relationship between the national and state parties that has had a profound effect on the party system. These trends include: (1) a weakening of the party role in presidential nominating politics; (2) a nationalizing tendency within the party organizations that has seriously affected the traditional decentralization; (3) an increasing role for campaign technicians, experts, and private consultants who operate outside the framework of the party organizations; (4) a series of changes in the way campaigns are funded and campaign finance is regulated; and (5) an important strengthening of the state party organizations. Some of these changes have appeared to weaken the state party organizations while others would seem to have strengthened them. Regardless of their ultimate effect, however, this second wave of post–1960 reforms has had a remarkable impact upon the power relationship among the levels of the party organizations.

STATE PARTIES AND PRESIDENTIAL NOMINATIONS

Parties have always had to compete with other forces—interest groups, candidate organizations, political action committees, campaign consultants, and media experts—for influence in the political process. But it has been the nomination of candidates for public office that most observers have emphasized as being crucial to the meaningful functioning of parties. In his treatise on parties referred to earlier, Professor Schattschneider stated, "Unless the party

makes authoritative nominations, it cannot stay in business. . . .
The nature of the nominating procedure determines the nature
of the party; he who can make nominations is the owner of the
party."

Until the 1970s, the parties did control presidential nominations. Most national convention delegates were chosen not by
primaries, but by state and district caucuses and conventions run
by the parties. Party organizational leaders tended to dominate
this process of delegate selection. Most attempts to influence the
delegates' candidate preference were made after they had been
selected by the party caucuses or state conventions. To influence
these delegates, a presidential candidate or his organization leaders had to have a great deal of political intelligence about state
party organizations. Knowing the party leadership in the states
was a particular advantage in the quest for a nomination, as with
James E. Farley's remarkable facility for remembering and recognizing local party leaders during his national tour in search of
delegates for Franklin D. Roosevelt. In later years, presidential
aspirants like Hubert Humphrey, Richard Nixon, and Barry
Goldwater had a head start over their competition because they
had traveled extensively and given assistance to state and local
party leaders over a period of years. They knew which state and
local party leaders could be called upon to furnish needed information and support. Presidential scholar Richard Neustadt
has called the pre–1970s period of presidential nominations the
"age of the barons" when "in each major party some fifty to one
hundred men—state leaders, local bosses, elder statesmen, big
contributors—decided nominations."

The few presidential primaries that did exist (fifteen in 1952)
did not dominate the process. Rather, primaries were important
largely because they represented a reasonably objective indicator
of a candidate's vote-getting ability. The front running candidates
tended to avoid primaries, unless they were certain of victory. A
bad showing could be interpreted as evidence that the candidate
was unelectable and result in a loss of existing support. The
primary, therefore, was important to candidates who were either
far behind or who had severe handicaps to overcome. One such
candidate was John F. Kennedy in 1960, whose Catholicism was
thought by party leaders to be a major liability. His impressive
primary victory in heavily Protestant West Virginia, however,

helped to quiet concerns about the religious issue. Similarly, in 1968 Nixon needed primary wins to dispel his image as a loser after his loss of the Presidency in 1960 and the California governorship in 1962. Primary victories could be used to gain leverage in bargaining with state and local party leaders, who controlled state delegations. But as Adlai Stevenson in 1952 and Hubert Humphrey in 1968 demonstrated when they won Democratic nominations without seriously contesting the primaries, state and local party organization support was indispensable.

If the first sixty years of this century were the "age of the barons," as Neustadt pointed out, the 1970s and 1980s were the "age of the candidate." No longer were most delegates chosen via party-dominated caucuses and conventions. In 1980, thirty-seven states used presidential primaries and over 75 percent of the delegates were selected where a primary was in use. Presidential primaries place a premium on media exposure, direct appeals to voters, canvassing by zealous volunteers, and personal candidate organizations—not on support by party leaders. The early primaries—especially the one in New Hampshire—have come to have a decisive influence upon the outcome of the nomination contest.

Even in those states that have retained the caucus/convention method of delegate selection, the role of party leaders has been diminished. Rules changes mandating open and participatory procedures, especially in the Democratic party, have relegated state party leaders to a minor role, and candidate organizations have come to dominate the process. Limits on contributions to presidential candidates and the availability of federal matching grants (under the Federal Election Campaign Act) to finance nomination campaigns have also diminished the influence of large contributors to the parties.

The presidential nomination process of the 1980s has so little regular party involvement that Austin Ranney of the American Enterprise Institute has suggested that it is "something approaching a no-party system" in which "party organizations simply are not actors in presidential politics. Indeed, they are little more than custodians of the party-label prize which goes to the winning candidate organization. The parties have long since ceased to be the judges *awarding* the prize."

Most observers believe that the evolution of the presidential nominating system from an exclusively party process into a primary-centered and candidate-dominated process has had profound and adverse consequences for the political leadership of the nation. These include:

1. nomination of candidates with limited experience in national politics and international affairs;
2. nomination of candidates who have not been screened and assessed by their peers, men and women who have observed and evaluated the aspirants at close range over a period of time; and
3. excessively long nomination campaigns that involve heavy wear and tear on the candidates and their families and may exclude from the competition incumbent officeholders with major governing responsibilities.

Under the pre–1970s process of presidential nominations, these problems were reduced because primaries were important primarily as a means of testing the electability of presidential hopefuls, and candidates still had to pass muster before the organizational leaders of their party. The power of these organizational leaders, who could exercise peer review over the candidates, was highlighted by David Broder when he compared John F. Kennedy's pathway to the nomination with that of Jimmy Carter.

> Kennedy ran in four contested primaries. Contrast that with the thirty-five that await anyone who wants the nomination in 1980. After Kennedy won in West Virginia, he still had to persuade the leaders of his party . . . that they could stake their reputation on his qualities as the best man to be the standard bearer of the party. Contrast that with Jimmy Carter, who never had to meet, and in fact, in many cases did not meet, those similar officials until after he had achieved the Democratic nomination.

Successful presidential nominees selected via the party-dominated process took office with alliances that made it possible for them to organize the coalitions necessary to lead a government. However, as Broder points out, with the nominating system in place for the 1980s, the President emerges

> as a fellow whose only coalition is whatever he got out of the living rooms in Iowa. If there is one thing that Jimmy Carter's frustration in office ought to teach us, it is that the affiliation and commitment that is made on Iowa caucus night and New Hampshire primary day is not by itself sufficient to sustain a man for four years in the White House.

A system which encourages the candidate to create a campaign organization devoted exclusively to his candidacy, to appeal di-

rectly to an unorganized electorate via the media, and to forgo
traditional party networks thus creates the danger that a new
President may find himself isolated from those needed to form
an effective government and to build the coalitions necessary
to implement his policies. A case in point is the Presidency of
Jimmy Carter, who sought to govern using many of the same
techniques that had served him so well as a candidate for the
nomination. As President, he continued to remain aloof from
the leaders of the Washington community, the state parties, and
the interest groups, while maintaining an outsider image and
making frequent direct television appeals to the electorate.
History, we are confident, will record that this was a leadership
style that proved inadequate to the task of governance.

Whatever the defects of the presidential nomination system,
it should be pointed out that as this process came to be primary-
centered and dominated by candidate organizations in the 1960s
and 1970s, it has been brought into conformity with the nomination process for other state and federal offices. Since Wisconsin
enacted the first direct primary law at the turn of the century,
the states have increasingly developed nomination procedures
that have weakened the capacity of state parties to dominate the
selection of candidates. It can, therefore, be argued that we are
in the final stages of a process that has finally brought presidential
nominations into harmony with the general pattern of nominations in the states. The durability of the direct primary at the
state level, in spite of its acknowledged party-weakening effects,
argues persuasively against any likely reversal of the trend toward
open and participatory delegate selection procedures.

The tendency toward weakened party control of nominations—
both federal and state—must, however, be considered in its larger
context. As political scientist James Q. Wilson has pointed out,
one of the most important trends of the twentieth century has
been the disaggregation of American politics—the weakening of
the capacity of leaders to assemble and wield power within and
among political institutions. The weakening of parties via the
primary method of nomination is but one example. Within the
executive branch, the spread of the civil service system, the tendency of the far-flung bureaucracy to be captured by its clientele,
and the diverse "issue networks" composed of specialists in selected
areas have all conspired to severely limit presidential power.

Similarly, the record of Congress in this century, starting with the revolt against House Speaker Joseph Cannon in 1910–11 and continuing down through the efforts of the reformers of the 1970s to weaken the committee chairmen and distribute power to the subcommittees, suggests the pervasiveness of the trend away from aggregated power within American political institutions. Therefore, those who wish to strengthen presidential leadership by reinjecting state party leaders into the nomination process should recognize that they are swimming against the current of twentieth century political trends. The American culture has always been suspicious of strong political parties, and there is no evidence that this predisposition is changing.

If the traditional confederate structure of state and local party leaders has seen its influence over presidential nominations diminish, the new presidential politics does include a positive party development. As political scientist Leon Epstein has pointed out, there has developed a "presidential party"—the "national following of activists gathered about a candidate." While these organizations are more ad hoc than conventional party organizations, they do have considerable continuity from one campaign to another, e.g., the conservatives who were first activated for Goldwater continued their involvement, including the holding of party office, and were enlisted into the Reagan campaigns of 1976 and 1980. Similarly, liberal activists from the 1956 Stevenson and 1960 Kennedy campaigns became a part of the Eugene McCarthy and Robert Kennedy campaigns in 1968. John Kessel's analyses of presidential campaigns have revealed that these "presidential party" activists are strongly issue-oriented. These "parties" are also more national in character than the traditional party organizations. Even though there is a natural reluctance to think of these "presidential parties" as political parties, Epstein is correct in asserting that they do perform some of the functions of parties. Like conventional parties, they also have both national and state leadership strata.

Because they are national in scope, exhibit continuing interest and involvement in politics, and are issue-oriented, these "presidential parties" are a resource that can be used by Presidents in mobilizing support for their programs. For example, during the Reagan administration's uphill struggle to prevent a congressional veto of the projected sale of AWACS planes to Saudi

Arabia, the "presidential party" network of Reagan-Bush state campaign committees was activated to contact its followers, who were asked in turn to urge their senators to support the President's position on the AWACS sale.

It should be noted that the presidential nominating process continues to be in a state of flux. Since 1972, when the McGovern-Fraser commission reforms took effect within the Democratic party, each succeeding presidential nomination contest has been fought under a different set of rules. The 1984 nominations promise to be no exception. Both the Republican National Committee and the Democratic National Committee appointed committees to review the nomination procedures after the 1980 elections. Although the RNC has shown little interest in major changes, the DNC's Commission on Presidential Nominations, chaired by Governor James B. Hunt of North Carolina, proposed major revisions. These include shortening the primary season and granting uncommitted delegate status to a large group of party and elected officials, including two-thirds of House and Senate members, who would be selected by their respective party caucuses. Whatever the merits of this plan to gain greater public official participation in presidential selection, it is likely to further diminish the role of state parties. A large and potentially influential block of delegates under the Hunt commission plan would be chosen, not by state parties or state primary electorates, but by congressional and senatorial caucuses.

NATIONALIZING TRENDS IN THE AMERICAN PARTY SYSTEM

If a consistent theme has run through the political science literature on American political parties, it has been their decentralized power structures—weak national party organization with the focus of strength residing in state and local units. Various changes have taken place in the post–World War II period that have caused political scientists to reassess the decentralization concept and to recognize substantial trends toward nationalization. The national parties during this period have increased their control over the state parties. In the case of the Democrats, this process has been closely associated with the new presidential politics which we have just discussed. Since the Dixiecrat insurrection within the Democratic party in 1948, the national party has been involved in enforcing rules on the state parties to assure loyalty to the presidential ticket. Following the divisive 1968 Democratic National Convention, the Democratic party, through a series of reform commissions starting with the Mc-Govern-Frazer commission and continuing through the Hunt commission, totally revamped the national party rules, especially as they pertained to delegate selection. These reform rules set forth an elaborate set of delegate selection procedures that the state parties were required to follow. In addition, the National Democratic Charter adopted in 1974 contains stipulations concerning how state parties shall be organized and function.

The post–1968 rules of the national Democratic party banned the open primary and the use of the unit rule at conventions. They also specified enforceable guidelines for the timing and openness of delegate selection procedures; proportional representation within state delegations of the primary and caucus participants' candidate preferences; representation of women, youth, and minorities; and other procedures previously determined by state party rules or state statutes. Following the approval of these guidelines, the DNC moved aggressively to enforce the rules upon state parties. The power of the DNC to require compliance with its rules has been upheld in a series of U.S. Supreme Court decisions. The Democratic party has, therefore, been nationalized and the old hegemony of the state parties broken, at least in the area of delegate selection.

The consequences of the post–1968 rules for the Democratic party are profound. Austin Ranney believes that as a result of these rules, the national party's "power to make rules governing presidential nominating processes is, in both reality and legal principle, at its highest peak by far since the 1820s." What is not clear is whether the heavy investment of national party resources in the stringent enforcement of national party rules upon state parties has strengthened the Democratic party in the states. The meager resources of the DNC have been used to monitor and regulate the state parties. The state parties in turn have been forced to spend time, personnel, and treasure developing procedures that conform to national party rules, some of which are offensive to political leaders and voters in the various states (for example, requiring Wisconsin to abandon its tradition of open presidential primaries). Since these rule-enforcement activ-

ities are peripheral to the parties' central responsibility of electing candidates, it can be argued that the nationalizing process
within the Democratic party has weakened the party's capacity to
mobilize support for its candidates or incumbent officeholders.

The nationalization process within the Republican party has
been of a quite different nature. Although the Republicans did
follow the lead of the Democrats in appointing committees to
suggest changes in the party's delegate selection procedures, the
party deliberately rejected any delegate selection procedures that
would have altered the confederate character of the party's legal
structure governing the relations between the national and state
parties. Instead of emphasizing *procedural reform* after the pattern of the Democrats, the Republican National Committee's
enhanced power has been achieved through *organizational reform*
—providing extensive services to state party organizations and
candidates. Increased interdependence between national and state
parties has thereby been gained through the provision of services
instead of through legal sanctions.

The RNC started this program in a modest way during the
chairmanship of Ray C. Bliss (1965–69). It was expanded in an
unprecedented manner by Chairman Bill Brock (1977–81), who
believed that the party could be strengthened most effectively by
shoring up its state and local base. Brock's organizational reform
program involved regional political directors appointed to work
with state parties in their regions; regional finance directors to
give technical assistance in fund raising; a sophisticated data
processing network to provide computer services to state parties
at minimal cost; a local elections division which provides technical, staff, and financial assistance to the state legislative campaigns;
assistance developing congressional and legislative redistricting
plans; and financial support for gubernatorial and state legislative candidates. The magnitude of these efforts can be seen
in the following measures of support given to candidates by the
RNC's Local Elections Division in 1980:

- Conducted 96 seminars to train 5,000 candidates.
- Conducted 210 public opinion surveys for selected candidates.
- Worked directly with 4,000 candidates.
- Made direct contributions of $1.7 million to candidates.

The nationalizing process in the GOP has also affected senatorial and congressional elections. The national party presence

in these previously state and local party affairs is substantial. The RNC has worked closely with the National Republican Congressional Committee in its efforts to recruit, train, support, and finance Republican congressional candidates. In 1980 the RNC spent $1.1 million in cash and in-kind contributions to support 138 candidates in specially targeted districts. The RNC also worked with the National Republican Senatorial Committee to provide $400,000 in financial and technical assistance to senatorial candidates in 1980. A major RNC expenditure in 1980 was a $9.4 million national advertising campaign for all Republican candidates.

With its highly successful fund-raising program to support these programs, the RNC has gained an enlarged role in the political system. There is now much more interdependence between the national and state parties and between the national party and GOP candidates or officeholders than there was prior to the initiation of Brock's program. The RNC has interjected itself into the organizational and the campaign activities of the state parties. As a result, the GOP is organizationally a stronger party than the Democrats who have chosen to emphasize procedural reform. The Republican organizational strength has been used primarily for electioneering. If the nationalizing trends within the party continue, however, the potential exists for the better integrated Republican party to use its resources for such noncampaign functions as mobilizing support for the programs of Republican Presidents. There were some indications in 1981 that this is already beginning to occur.

Like most Presidents, Ronald Reagan has moved to assert control of his party's national committee through the designation of its chairman and a regular liaison process between the White House political office and the RNC. But unlike many of his predecessors, President Reagan gives no evidence that he intends to ignore or downgrade his party's national committee the way Presidents Kennedy, Johnson, Nixon, and Carter did. Indeed, the RNC has been used to build support for the President's program in a major way. In 1981, the RNC spent more than $900,000 on public opinion surveys to help assess public attitudes toward the President and his programs. During congressional consideration of the President's budget proposals in the spring of 1981, the RNC dispatched two dozen officials—including Vice President Bush, Office of Management and Budget Director David Stockman, former President Ford, and over twenty members of Congress to the districts of sixty-two targeted Democratic House members whom the Republicans hoped could be persuaded to support the President's budget. The RNC also culled from the public record of the Federal Election Commission the names of persons and organizations that supported both Reagan and conservative Democratic members of Congress and urged these people to encourage their representatives to support the President's program. During the drive to gain congressional approval of the President's tax reduction program, the RNC launched a $500,000 national radio advertising campaign which concentrated on selected media markets where, it was thought, the ads might influence the votes of Democratic members of Congress.

Such national party activities in support of their President's policies suggest that party organizations can usefully augment the resources of the White House in gaining public and congressional support. The state party organizations, however, have not participated actively in this process, though it is quite possible that the better organized Republican state organizations could make a contribution in mobilizing support for a President. Nevertheless, the overall trend toward nationalization, particularly in the Democratic party, has been the second factor to have a negative impact on the state party organizations.

CAMPAIGNING OUTSIDE THE PARTY APPARATUS

Achieving a preeminent role in campaigns has always been difficult for American parties. Federalism has not only fragmented the party organizations, it also has meant that literally thousands of party candidates run for public office. The sheer size of the campaign enterprise plus the frequency of American elections imposes an almost impossible campaign burden upon even the most efficient of party organizations. Furthermore, parties are not the only actors in the campaign process. They have always had to compete with other forces—candidate organizations, campaign managers, and interest groups. In recent years, the ability of the parties to compete for a place in the campaign process has been adversely affected by the growth of a professional corps of campaign experts and consultants skilled in the latest campaign techniques and technology. These professionals operate largely outside the party organizations, are closely tied to individual candidates, and pose a mounting threat to the influence of the parties.

Robert Agranoff, a political scientist who has studied changes in campaign styles and is himself one of the new breed of campaign professionals, points out four important distinctions between the "old" style of campaigning and the "new" style. First, the candidate, rather than the party, tends to be the major focus of modern campaigns. A well-financed candidate can build an organization devoted almost exclusively to his own election, while the traditional party support was usually divided between many candidates for many offices. Even though there are campaigns which are still run by party organizations, most have given way to candidate-directed campaigns, often carried out by professional managers outside the party apparatus.

Second, in the new modes of campaigning that have emerged in the past three decades, the use of party professionals has given way to the technical professional—the management specialist, the pollster, the direct mail expert, and the media consultant. As it became evident that the traditional party organizations usually did not have personnel trained in these new campaign techniques, candidates turned more and more to those who did have such skills.

A third distinction between the "old" and "new" styles of campaign management stems from improvements in technology. The new campaign manager uses information gathered systematically from public opinion surveys, census tracts, precinct voting records, and poll lists and processes this data through a computer. As a result, the traditional reliance on precinct captains and party officials for needed information has been substantially reduced.

The fourth change has emerged from the communications revolution. In earlier times information was distributed to the voters through speeches, rallies, and handouts organized by the political party. Services and favors were the staples of the precinct captain. The party leader cut through government bureaucracy, found jobs, and performed favors. The payoff was on election day when the voters were asked to reciprocate for past favors. Now, the candidate-oriented campaign is often guided by outside experts who have mastered the use of telephone banks, computer-printed direct mail letters, and radio and television advertising. The key to all of these changes, Agranoff notes, is the transfer of campaign emphasis from political party organization to candidate organization. The transfer was made possible by the development of modern communications and computer technology.

The "old" politics of party-directed campaigns still occupies a place in the contests for offices below the congressional and statewide levels, in a few major cities, and some sparsely populated areas. Candidates for major office, however, wishing to maximize their chances for election, increasingly embrace the new technology and professional management even though this has undercut the traditional campaign role of the party.

The Electronic Media and Politics—Television has supplanted the political party as the principal conduit between the candidates and voters. It represents a powerful way to reach masses of voters and affect their election decisions. The rise of television has occurred at a time when the role of parties in presidential nominations has been diminished as a result of increased use of presidential primaries and the reforms of the 1970s. As a consequence, the media's influence on the selection of candidates has been enhanced. One of the reasons that the Iowa caucuses and the New Hampshire primary early in the presidential nomination season are perceived as being so important is that they offer the first opportunity for the television media to begin the process of electing front runners and discarding those who are seen to be also-rans. These early calculations, according to R. W. Apple of the *New York Times*, "have a life of their own, because they are the backdrop against which politicians and the media tend to measure the performance of the various candidates in their early confrontations."

In 1976 Jimmy Carter emerged from obscurity largely because the media coverage of him was pervasive and favorable. He was a different kind of candidate, from a southern state, and was successful in demonstrating through television that he was intelligent, could not be tied to recent scandalous events in Washington or to the Vietnam War, and he quickly became the man to beat for the nomination. Furthermore, as has been noted by some scholars who have studied the campaign, he won his front runner's status after only about 5 percent of the national convention delegates had been chosen. Momentum then was on his side. Therefore, on the basis of thirty years of experience with television and politics, particularly at the presidential level, it is reasonably safe to say that the electronic media have demonstrated a growing ability to influence nominations and to help determine those who will drop by the wayside. The same can be said of the impact of television on campaigns in the states.

A second major aspect of the new politics is that the mass media, particularly television, have become important determinants as to the kinds of campaigns that will be waged. Candidates now gauge their campaign activities to media opportunities and concentrate attention on press conferences and photo opportunities. Public appearances and press releases are timed to meet television and press deadlines for the evening news. When it became apparent in 1976 that the Iowa caucuses were going to be heavily covered by the media, candidates who had previously shown no interest in Iowa hastily rearranged their schedules so that they could hopefully make a good showing in that state.

Candidates who are not good public speakers are scheduled and filmed with small groups of voters with whom they can interact. Others, who are unable to attract media attention, stage events which they hope will gain them air time and column inches. Visiting the factory gate, walking across the state, working for a day as an ordinary laborer, going up in a balloon or down in a diving suit, have all become staples of the media campaign. They are particularly important to nonincumbents who must scramble for attention and do not have the built-in advantages offered to incumbent officeholders.

Finally, the third major impact of the media on politics has been the decline in influence of the political parties, particularly in elections for Presidents. Professor Doris Graber has noted that when social scientists first studied the impact of the mass media on the outcome of 1940s presidential elections they concluded that party allegiance was the most important determining factor in the vote, followed by group allegiance, the candidate's personality, and the consideration of issues. With the advent of the television age, however, the order has been reversed with the personality of the candidate becoming the principal determinant, and issues, party affiliation, and group membership following in order. As she notes, when the voters base their decisions on candidate personality and issues, the media, particularly television, become more important because they represent the chief source of information about such matters. Correspondingly, since this has been a traditional role of the political parties, they become less important in the voter equation. Even so, party affiliation remains an important determinant of voting behavior in state and local elections where the large number of candidates makes it more likely that voters will rely on the party in its traditional cue-giving role. When party cues are lacking, however, voters are more likely to rely on the electronic and print media in making candidate and issue choices.

All in all, therefore, the emergence of the electronic media has brought with it a different type of candidate, a new style of campaigning, and an erosion of influence for the political parties. Television in particular has assumed an important place in the kinds of decisions made by the electorate. It is an awesome power, but it is one that concentrates on major candidates—Presidents, governors, senators, and, on occasion, members of Congress. It is no wonder that the professional media adviser and the experienced campaign consultant have assumed roles of such importance in major political campaigns.

The Impact of Technology on Politics—Not long after the invention of the computer some far-sighted political leaders sensed the value of automatic data processing in party organizational activities and campaigns. As early as 1966, the RNC authorized a study of centralized data processing and produced and distributed a handbook to explain computer technology in lay terms. It also undertook a pilot program based on test precincts and sponsored some training conferences designed to familiarize state party leaders with the use of such equipment.

Decision makers in a political campaign need to know the economic, social, and political composition of the electorate to whom they are directing their appeal. They need to be able to pinpoint what issues are important and where their significance lies within their constituency. Up-to-date precinct lists, which in many states can be purchased from voter registrars, are important to "get-out-the-vote" drives and to direct mail fund raising. Campaign strategists know that there is no effective way to reach all of the voters. Information on selected voter groups, however, is available through computer technology, and it has become commonplace in major campaigns for a voter profile to be constructed based on census data, past voting records, and various economic indicators. All of these are suitable for computerization and, in fact, could not efficiently be provided in any other way.

The wide array of campaign uses for data processing has caused an increasing number of candidates for major office to use this technology as a matter of course. Since data processing services are normally provided not by state and local party organizations but by campaign consultants, these professionals have gained prominence in campaigns.

The Impact of Professional Campaign Management—Private firms specializing in campaign consulting and management are a growth industry in the 1980s. Agranoff has listed twenty-seven different categories of consultants that a candidate might employ. The scope of available activities is impressive—from specialists in campaign planning, fund raising, and direct mail through media consultants. Again, though, the political parties are for the most part by-passed as the candidates for major offices hire their own consultants, campaign managers, and support service firms to plan and carry out their campaigns. These are candidate-centered campaigns that concentrate on effective use of the media, public opinion polling, advertising, and demographic analysis of voter groups. The professional consultants who organize these campaigns are usually attempting to achieve scientifically what old-time party strategists sought to do by common sense and conventional wisdom. It has been noted by some students that media experts and professional managers are often trying to shape the views of the public to fit the client-candidate, while the traditional campaign managers are trying to use party resources to mobilize preexisting sentiments and to capitalize on identified party members. Even when there is an attempt to blend both kinds of campaigns, it is often not an easy marriage. The new specialists are apt to believe that the politicians are misdirecting their energies and wasting their time; the political managers are likely to view the campaign "scientists" with distrust and condescension. Most major candidates, however, opt for the professionally managed campaign organized and run by technologists. As John Herbers, writing in the *New York Times*, noted, a number of key Republican candidates for President in 1980 did not attend the semiannual meeting of the RNC (including Ronald Reagan, John Connally, and Howard Baker, Jr.) because "although those who stayed away gave various reasons for doing so, some party leaders said the contenders were so busy setting up organizations outside the party that they saw little point in making personal appeals to the regular party leaders."

There is no question that the increasing use of the combination of the electronic media, automatic data processing, and professional campaign consultants has undercut the traditional campaign role of political parties and affected our institutions of government. Reliance on campaign consultants and media campaigns, with their direct appeals to the voters over the heads of party and group leaders, is not geared toward negotiation, compromise, and coalition building. Rather, media campaigns are often heavily symbolic, necessarily superficial in the handling of issues, and often confrontational in character. But governing requires more than symbolic appeals and confrontations. It demands coalition building—the traditional function of political parties. However, to the extent that changes in campaign practices by-pass parties and result in candidates with less experience in this art, our governing institutions are likely to be staffed by personnel who will have to learn these skills through on-the-job training.

CAMPAIGN FINANCE, PACS, AND THE STATE PARTIES

The role of the state parties in influencing national political leadership has been affected significantly by changes in campaign finance legislation, especially by the enactment of the Federal Election Campaign Act of 1971 (FECA) and the subsequent amendments to the act in 1974, 1976, and 1979. Because of the restrictions on the amount of money that state and local party organizations can contribute to federal candidates under this legislation, the state parties have been rather effectively excluded from a major role in financing the campaigns of federal candidates. At the same time, the FECA encourages the creation of political action committees (PACs)—a major competitor of the parties for political influence.

Financing the Presidential Campaign—The FECA makes major presidential party candidates eligible for public funding ($29.4 million in 1980) in their general election campaigns on the condition that they accept no outside contributions. Since 1976, when this provision of the act first went into effect, all major party candidates have accepted public funding, and 1984 nominees are expected to follow the example of Ford, Carter, and Reagan. In addition to the public subsidy, the Republican and Democratic National Committees are also permitted to fund their party's presidential ticket ($4.6 million in 1980).

The experience with the act in 1976 was one of discouraging state and local party activity in support of the presidential candidates. The general election campaign operated under an expenditure ceiling imposed as a condition for receiving the public subsidy. Centralized control of expenditures was required, and state and local organizational activities were discouraged in favor of media expenditures. Republican Congressman Richard Cheney of Wyoming, formerly President Ford's White House chief of staff, explained the effect of the public subsidy and expenditure limits as follows:

> . . . in the general election, because no contributions are permitted once federal funds become available for the fall campaign, it is even more important to discourage such [grass-roots organizations] activity. . . . It was much easier . . . to spend money on identifiable goods and services such as electronic media and production costs . . . than it was to spend it intelligently on social and state organizational efforts. . . .

The discouragement of state and local party involvement in presidential campaigns was eased somewhat for the 1980 election when Congress authorized state and local parties to spend money on local organizing and voter mobilization activities. The superior organizational and financial resources of the Republican state and local organizations were apparent in the expenditures reported to the Federal Election Commission. Republican state and local parties spent $15 million to support the Reagan-Bush ticket, while state and local Democratic organizations spent only $5 million for Carter and Mondale.

Financing Congressional Campaigns—In congressional and senatorial elections, the role of state and local parties has also been limited by the FECA. The act imposes expenditure and contribution limits on the support that can be provided by parties to candidates. As a result, congressional and senatorial candidates must rely heavily on nonparty sources for funds. Therefore, representatives and senators, once in office, feel little sense of obligation to their state and local parties, and the parties lack significant influence on the behavior of legislators in the halls of Congress.

A campaign finance practice that threatens to further lessen the involvement of state and local parties in congressional and senatorial elections is the "agency agreement" between national party committees and state parties. As practiced by the National Republican Senatorial Committee (NRSC) and participating Republican state parties, this technique has enabled the NRSC to act as the surrogate of the state parties in senatorial races and thereby spend not only its own legal limit but also that of the state party, thus increasing the legal spending entitlement of the national party committee. Over the objections of Democratic leaders, who challenged this practice, both the Federal Election Commission and the United States Supreme Court have upheld the "agency agreement" practice which enabled the NRSC to contribute $2.7 million to candidates in 1980. While this practice further weakens the influence of state parties over their senators, it does mean that the national party organizations can play a greater role in financing congressional and senatorial candidates. It is, therefore, possible that legislators, elected with the substantial national party support that the "agency agreement" facilitates, may pay greater attention to national party and presidential policy initiatives. It also constitutes additional evidence of the trend toward nationalization of the party organizations.

Political Action Committees—Another major consequence of the Federal Election Campaign Act has been its encouragement of political action committees. The PAC is a type of "political committee" defined by statute and given the right to solicit and distribute funds to candidates. Corporate PACs constitute an exception to the statutory prohibition against contributions by corporations to federal campaigns. Corporations under the FECA may use company funds to defray the administration expenses of establishing PACs and soliciting contributions from stockholders, executives, and their families. Labor union and trade association PACs are also recognized by the law and restricted to soliciting funds from their members. Prior to the legal recognition of PACs in the 1971 FECA, they were primarily a labor union phenomenon, with the AFL-CIO's Committee on Political Education (COPE) functioning as the leader in the field. Once the legal way was cleared for corporate PACs, their number increased dramatically so that by 1978 there were 784 of them; at the same time there were 218 labor PACs and 631 that were organized on other bases. With escalating campaign costs, PACs have become an increasingly important source of campaign funds, particularly for congressional candidates. For example, 25 percent of the $92.2 million raised to support House candidates in 1978 came from PACs, compared to 14 percent of the $38.9 million collected for congressional aspirants in 1972. By contrast, the role of parties in financing House races has diminished. Party contributions were 7 percent of the total raised in 1978, compared to the 17 percent the parties collected in 1972.

While PAC growth is normally considered evidence of the decline of parties, it is not yet clear that the increased scope of PAC activities necessarily weakened parties. Both the national Republican and Democratic parties have sought to relate their activities to those of the PACs and to coordinate PAC activity in support of party candidates. The party organizations can, therefore, become a mechanism for focusing and coordinating the efforts of PACs to influence the outcome of elections. Such party activities, already underway at the national level and possibly in the future at the state level, could enhance the influence of party organizations upon congressional and senatorial campaigns.

THE STRENGTHENING OF STATE PARTY ORGANIZATIONS

The four trends previously discussed have generally reduced the state party role in presidential nominations and general election campaigns, and in the process they diminished party influence in officeholders. But paradoxically, while these trends have been progressing, state parties have developed stronger and more professional headquarters operations.

It had been difficult to study state parties systematically in the past because of their widespread geographical distribution, their notorious failure to maintain the continuity of official records, and the rapid changes in fortune that beset them due to the ups and downs of the electoral process. Even so, a body of comparative literature covering a considerable period of time has now been developed, and it has permitted us to track a remarkable pattern of organizational growth and political sophistication. Most of this change has occurred since the early 1960s.

Many political scientists and practitioners believe that a strong state party headquarters operation is essential to the electoral success or failure of a political party. Strong organizations offer the capability for systematic fund raising, professional research and public relations, improved recruitment of candidates, and increased campaign services, all of which are elements of successful campaigns. Furthermore, party control of such services enables the parties to compete with outside consulting firms for a role in the campaign process. Just as clearly, organized party activities do not guarantee electoral success; even the best party organization suffers election losses. But a strong state party operating under effective leadership, with a regular source of funds, can offer a better chance for success.

There has been little agreement on which organizational attributes truly constitute the ingredients of political strength. Intuitively, though, strong parties are those which are able to maintain a permanent headquarters, provide a steady source of operating funds, and enjoy the services of a professional staff.

Maintaining a State Party Headquarters—Most of the state parties today maintain a party headquarters in a permanent location (usually the state capital) on a regular basis. A headquarters should be the nerve center of a political party, the focal point for recruitment, campaign strategy, public opinion polling and analysis, patronage, clearance, research, fund raising, data processing, public relations, and the coordination of party activities among the levels of the party hierarchy. One study found that in the mid–1970s only ten of the one hundred state parties did not have a state headquarters, a considerable improvement over 1960 when only half of them did. At the present time all but five state parties maintain a headquarters on a regular basis. Some are not well funded, are understaffed, and see their fortunes improve or decline according to the outcome of the last election, but their mere existence demonstrates a growing recognition of their importance to party building.

Providing a Regular Source of Operating Funds—Operating funds are the most important single ingredient in the maintenance of a state party headquarters. The rent or mortgage payment must be made, staff salaries covered, and the expenses of communications, copy systems, capital outlay, and day-to-day operations provided. On occasion, a particularly devastating electoral defeat may cause contributions to dry up and force the closing of the state headquarters, but in virtually every case its reopening is made a first priority for the continued growth of the party.

The operation of a state headquarters is usually dependent upon a regular and trustworthy source of funds. There are several traditional sources of operating and campaign funds available to the parties, as well as some new ones just now coming into vogue. Small contributor programs based on computerization and direct mail have been successful in a number of states. Most have been built upon the foundation laid by the Republican National Committee with its pioneering effort in the 1960s to raise large sums of money in small amounts.

Large contributor programs (governors' clubs, century clubs, etc.), dinners, telethons, receptions, and other special events have developed to improve the fiscal health of the state parties. A few state parties still get money from various kinds of patronage programs, although the growth of civil service systems and merit systems during the past half-century have undercut most of these efforts to collect political money from political appointees. The newest source of party funds is the growth of public funding programs in the states. In 1981, seventeen states had implemented public funding of campaigns. In eight states, the public funds are channeled through the parties for organizational purposes, candidate services, or cash contributions to candidates. In the remaining nine states, the bulk of the public money goes directly to candidates.

Regardless of the means used to raise money, the state parties must make a conscious decision to spend part of the funds that are garnered on party organizational activities and headquarters expenses. That has not always been the case. Most state fundraising drives have concentrated in the past on campaign finance —not money to support a more sophisticated party organization. The leaders in some state parties have, in fact, had a difficult time persuading their executive committees or county organizations that this was a proper or worthwhile use for contributions. The fact that most of them succeeded is attested to by the growth in operating budgets.

The average budget for the state parties in a 1979–80 sample of fifty-three state parties was $340,600. The smallest operating budget reported was $14,000 and the largest was $2.5 million. (Some of the data reported here are from a national study, funded by the National Science Foundation, of changes in the party system, presently being conducted by us and Professors Cornelius P. Cotter and James L. Gibson of the University of Wisconsin–Milwaukee.) These figures represent a dramatic increase since 1960 when the average state party operating budget was $188,125, although it should be noted that inflation was responsible for some of that increase. The major operating expense of a state party organization is staff salaries. Therefore, the degree of staffing is usually determined by the success of the fund-raising effort.

Staffing the Party Headquarters—A large majority of state parties are staffed by a full-time, salaried executive director. Over 90 percent of the party units have either an executive director or a full-time, paid state chairman or chairwoman. In both cases this represents a considerable growth from the 1960s when only 63 percent of the state party organizations had a full-time officer in charge. Even the support of a stable organizational cadre has not solved many of the problems of discontinuity that the state party organizations have. The tenure of state chairmen and women for the past thirty years has averaged slightly over two years. The coming and going of party leaders has had a deleterious effect on the party organizations in both program emphasis and continuity and in staff morale. Nevertheless, it must be assumed that a permanent paid staff, regardless of size and tenure in office, is better than no staff at all.

Since the 1960s there has been a gradual increase in the size of state headquarters' staffs so that in 1979–80 the average staff had approximately seven persons and 25 percent of them had ten or more. While staffs of this size permit a moderate amount of specialization, it is still necessary in most state headquarters for staffers to perform a variety of functions. The purpose of having a permanent headquarters, a regular source of funding, and a full-time staff is to carry out the functions normally ascribed to a political party. Political success is measured by electoral success, and the latter is often a product of the kind of services rendered by the state organization.

Services Offered by State Party Organizations—Party organizations exist to perform services of a political nature for constituent groups. The constituents of a party organization may be the candidates, incumbent office holders, local party organizations, or the voters. It is logical, therefore, that the kinds of activities carried on by the party organization are of two types: organization building and the needs of candidates. Organization building includes services provided by the party for the general good of the party. They are institutional support services such as fund raising, support for local organizations, the development of and leadership on issues, electoral mobilization, public opinion polling, public relations, and publications. Campaign services to candidates constitute the second major type of activity assumed by a party organization. They include advertising and media assistance, accounting and election law compliance, public opinion polling, research, voter registration and "get-out-the-vote" drives, campaign staffing, the publication and direct mail distribution of campaign literature, phone banks, fund raising, and campaign training seminars.

Obviously, the success of a state party in assuming this variety of activities depends on the quality of its leadership, the availability of funds and staff resources, and even its success in winning elections. Great variability exists among the state organizations in the number of these services that can be offered. About 90 percent conduct campaign seminars, but very few assist candidates with fund raising. About 50 percent offer some combination of these services.

The same pattern of variability exists in the area of organizational support. As we have seen, almost all of the state parties engage in some kind of organized fund-raising effort, and most of them operate an ongoing voter identification/registration/"get-out-the-vote" program. About 50 percent are involved in issue development, and nearly all publish literature and provide a newsletter or newspaper on a regular basis. The other organization building efforts are less widespread, but all are provided by some state parties.

The State Party Organizations in the American Party System— Organizational sophistication and growth have not automatically guaranteed greater success in winning state elections. The relationship between organizational strength and electoral success is complex and often indirect. Some minority parties, often in traditional one-party areas, e.g., the southern Republicans, may work for years to develop their organizational strength before it begins to pay off with election victories. Other state parties, even in highly competitive, two-party environments, have achieved substantial electoral success without highly developed party organizations. Over a period of time, however, the importance of organizational strength may be its role in providing an infrastructure for activists and candidates to continue to compete in the face of short-term defeats or enduring minority status.

In the context of the five important changes in the American party system that have occurred since World War II, it is clear that the growth and sophistication of the state party units has been the only one that has been of direct benefit to the state parties. The remaining four, presidential delegate selection processes, party nationalization, modern (and often nonparty) methods of campaigning, and changes in campaign finance practices, have tended to erode the influence of the state parties. In the long run, the ability of the state parties to maintain stronger organizations and to offer more sophisticated political services may be the key to a new kind of balance in the federal party structure.

American Political Parties: The Challenge to Survive

The changes in American politics in the second half of the twentieth century have not on the whole been kind to political parties. For those of us who believe in a strong two-party system, that is a hard fact to face. Seldom have so many changes come in such a brief period of time. The presidential nominating process is now candidate-dominated and primary-centered. Yet, given the persistence of the direct primary as a nominating device at the state and local levels, in spite of its acknowledged party-weakening effects, there is little reason to believe that there will be a reduction in the use of the presidential primary in the foreseeable future.

Campaign organizations built around candidates, run by private consulting firms, financed in some cases by public money and in others by political action committees, and centered on television exposure have reduced and restricted the role of the parties. There are many students of politics, scholars and practitioners alike, who believe that the parties are slowly disintegrating. But, paralleling these party-weakening events are some counter trends which may reflect continuing strength, viability, and durability of the parties. The most obvious of them is the increased organizational strength of the state parties which many believe to be the foundation of a strong party system. Even the growth of presidential parties composed of personal candidate organizations and the trend toward nationalization can have positive effects on the party system. The twenty years it has taken to build a strong Republican National Committee have paid off with an organizational capability that in some ways rivals those of the private consulting firms. Furthermore, the RNC's support of the state and local candidates and its efforts to provide sustenance to the lower units of the party are credited by many with a substantial share of credit for the GOP success in the 1980 elections.

Taken together, both the party-weakening trends and the party-strengthening trends suggest that state parties are unlikely to be a serious factor in the selection of national leaders anytime in the near future. It is also unlikely that they will be a factor permitting a President to undertake policy initiatives or to build coalitions of support based on them. It is more likely that the stronger, more virile state parties will be able to use their organizational resources to provide campaign services to state and local candidates (particularly those running for the state legislature) while supplementing the role of candidate organizations geared to congressional, senatorial, gubernatorial, and presidential elections.

Nevertheless, even though Presidents may not be able to rely on state party organizations for political strength or program support, it is possible, if the nationalization process continues, that the revitalized national party organizations will enable them to mobilize support for those programs. There is already considerable evidence of the impact that the RNC has had in building support for the policy initiatives of President Reagan.

The picture, then, is not necessarily a completely bleak one for the political parties. If these trends continue, they suggest that we may be moving from a confederate to a more federal type of party structure in which nonparty organizations play significant roles. Should this be the case, skilled incumbents may well be able to develop leadership and governing resources which permit parties to play a significant role in this new and changing environment.

As we concern ourselves with the present difficulties of effective governance facing national political leaders, there is a natural tendency to overstate the virtues of the old political order, when presidential politics was party-dominated, when congressional party discipline was strong, and when state and local parties played a greater role in the recruitment and nomination of candidates and in the general election campaign. Certainly in retrospect it appears that governance was facilitated by the old party system. The past era, however, also had its down side. The party-dominated presidential nominating process that produced an Abraham Lincoln, Woodrow Wilson, Franklin D. Roosevelt, and Dwight Eisenhower also gave us Warren Harding and John W. Davis. The tight discipline in Congress in the early days of this century was also characterized by "Cannonism" and "King Caucus." Party control of nominations and election campaigns at the state and local level frequently reflected bossism and violated the expectations that citizens had for open participation. Therefore, in our search for party-strengthening devices that will enhance the governing capacity of our leaders, we need to keep in mind the disadvantages associated with the era of stronger parties.

Most of us, however, could subscribe to a statement made by political scientist Thomas Cronin, a leading scholar of the Presidency, when he wrote

> A President attempting noble innovations . . . stands in great need of public support and, especially, of strong partisan backing. A partyless government is almost invariably an arbitrary and reactionary regime. This country has an extraordinary need for revitalized parties: first, to serve as instruments of support for, and to discipline the whims of, elected leaders; and, second, to serve as vehicles for the two-way communication of voter preferences and policy.

F. Christopher Arterton

4

Political Money and Party Strength

Surprise! Just when we had all learned to live with the reality and consequences of party decline, the very latest word from party scholars heralds a dramatic resurgence in party organizational strength. Relying primarily upon the fund-raising success of the Republican National Committee, both Xandra Kayden and David Adamany cautiously project current trends to arrive at a thesis of party revival. Similarly, researchers such as John Bibby and Robert Huckshorn, focusing upon party organizations at the state level, have recently reported that, surprisingly, they "are gaining in strength, rather than weakening."

This recent turnabout in our thinking about the future of political parties leads to a series of questions addressed in this chapter. What evidence exists for the party revival thesis? Is it unambiguous? To what degree can this revival be related to governmental policy, especially to the laws regulating election financing? Specifically, which provisions of the campaign laws appear

F. CHRISTOPHER ARTERTON *is associate professor in the Department of Political Science at Yale University. He is also chairman of the Faculty Study Group on Political Campaigns at the Institute of Politics at Harvard University. Dr. Arterton has written numerous papers and chapters in books on aspects of the electoral process and was editor of* An Analysis of the Impact of the Federal Election Campaign Act 1972–78 *for the U.S. House of Representatives. The author is indebted to David Mayhew and Gary Orren for their helpful comments on this essay.*

responsible for the recent development of financial strength of some party committees? To what degree do the current "revived parties" or currently "reviving parties" correspond to our traditional notions of political parties? Can these revived parties aid in the governing process by bridging the fragmentation of our formal governmental machinery? And, finally, if the answers to all these questions are favorable, to what degree can this trend be furthered by legislative amendments to the current campaign finance laws?

In seeking answers to these questions I have not engaged in extensive, first-hand field research on the state of American parties. Rather, I rely heavily upon the work of other scholars and journalists. The reader will find here an essay, not a research report. My intent is to stimulate thought and discussion and, perhaps, in the process, to point out gaps in our research which occur at critical points along the inquiry into the effectiveness and usefulness of parties. Since the thesis of party resurgence is based to some degree upon projections of current trends, clearly, continued attention to the state of our party committees is in order. But there are points at which detailed research findings could be very useful now. For example, while we can observe increased levels of party activity, we could be more confident if we could demonstrate some effect upon citizens or party office-holders. I hope as well to cast the hypothesis of party resurgence in a historical perspective. I will direct attention almost exclusively to the party presence in federal governance, although at points the discussion will digress into the realm of party organizations at the state level.

A Revival of the Grand Old Parties?

At the outset, we must clearly distinguish between parties as they have existed in our history on the national level from their organization and function in many states. Moving too swiftly across this divide can easily confound the analysis, for parties on the national level, except as legislative caucuses, have been historically largely a myth. As E. E. Schattschneider wrote forty years ago, "Decentralization of power is by all odds the most important single characteristic of the American political party." Schattschneider described national parties as merely "a loose confederation of state and local bosses for limited purposes." Similarly, writing just before a wave of rules changes altered forever the selection of convention delegates, Frank Sorauf, the most influential contemporary party scholar, observed, "Despite all the appearances of hierarchy in the American party organization, in no important way does any national party unit limit the autonomy of the state and local party organization."

Even the quadrennial nominating conventions should not be mythologized for more than they were: fragmented meetings of local party chieftains. Records of debate and voting at national conventions during the last century, for example, clearly reveal their nature as a political *process,* not as hierarchical and rational decision-making units. Far from being the ideal deliberating bodies, they were subject to all the irrationalities and momentary passions of any collective decision process, especially one compressed into a short time span. Where students of contemporary presidential nominations may complain, as Everett Carll Ladd, Jr. does, that "all the institutional parties do now is provide the setting for the actions of others," they imply a good deal more rationality—or "capacity to plan" as Ladd has argued elsewhere— than was ever present at the national level.

The principal distinction between the grand old party conventions and the present nominating system is in the number of actors whose collective behavior will determine the nomination. A few party leaders gathered together may well have been able to exercise greater judgment and prudence, or they may have brought a different range of evaluations. But they provide no guarantee of more rational decision making, precisely because national political parties have existed only on paper.

As for the enduring party organization, the national party committees never had an elaborate or sustained presence in Washington politics. They certainly were not deeply involved in congressional or senatorial elections, where state and local committees were often important. On the presidential level, the national committee generally remained a neutral host, rather than an active participant attempting to influence the outcomes.

To the extent that we now see national party organizations as major actors in federal elections, therefore, this development represents a change from, rather than a renewal of, the traditional party organization. The nature of this change, its implications for federal governance, and the extent to which the campaign finance laws constitute a driving force behind this growth, are the subjects for discussion in this chapter.

An Era of National Party Strength

The recent financial and organizational activity of the various party committees at the national level clearly demonstrates a level of party strength that is unexpected given the widespread alarms of party decline. In absolute terms, party committees raised and spent more funds in the 1980 elections than in any other contest in American history, and they had more employees engaged in more activities than ever before. Since, historically, campaigns were conducted through party committees, it is not really appropriate to compare whether the levels of party money and activity are a greater percentage now than they were traditionally. But it is fair to say that party money was a higher percentage of the total in 1980 than has been generally true since candidates gained financial independence sometime in the 1950s and 1960s.

What are the dimensions of this activity?

THE NATIONAL REPUBLICAN PARTY

The recent financial and organizational strength of the Republican party has been widely noted by journalists, politicians, and academicians. Accordingly, for the purposes of this discussion, only a brief recitation of their success is necessary.

At the national level, the Republican party is composed of three separate organizations, the national committee and the campaign committees for Senate and House candidates. All together these three committees raised over $100 million for the party effort in the 1980 elections. While each of these committees raises, spends, and contributes campaign funds separately, an important dimension to the recent success of the national Republican party has been the cooperation which has developed among these organizations. Instances of working relations include regular strategy meetings, sharing of funds to be thrown into important contests, and joint advertising campaigns. Even though they technically have a separate existence, for our purposes they can be referred to collectively as the national party organization.

The major engine driving the Republican success story has been the development of a large base of small contributors. By reinvesting large sums in direct mail lists, Republicans have been able to increase the number of regular contributors from around 35,000 in the early 1970s to more than 2 million by 1980. The average contribution was just under thirty dollars. All combined, the three national committees raised approximately $70 million for the 1980 elections in small contributions solicited through the mails.

The initial investment to establish a direct mail program is quite substantial; costs can absorb almost all of the proceeds. As the list of reliable contributors develops, however, these costs fall dramatically. Xandra Kayden reports that by 1980 the overhead for direct mail was around 20 percent, making it less expensive than all other means of raising party money.

Large donors are still courted and welcomed by the Republican party organizations; they provide about 33 percent of all receipts. But the success of the direct mail program has, for the first time, placed a national political party on a secure financial basis and given it ample disposable funds. Most of the newly discovered organizational strength of the Republicans can be traced to their ability to raise money.

Before passing on to examine what the Republicans did with all this money, we should note the less direct implications of the direct mail success. For the first time in American political history, there exists a substantial number of citizens who consider themselves to be *members* of a national party; they can carry cards in their wallets to prove it! This development is one aspect of the nationalization of the party system mentioned earlier. While we are still very far from a European conception of party membership, since one can opt into membership merely by making a contribution and no rights are attached, nevertheless, we should not ignore the fact that a concept of identity as "members" of a party, rather than as voters or identifiers, is developing.

During the 1980 elections, the Republican National Committee (RNC) spent $4.6 million on behalf of the Reagan-Bush ticket, the maximum permitted by the Federal Election Campaign Act (FECA). And, during 1979 and 1980, the committee contributed at least another $6 million in cash or "in-kind" support to candi-

dates running in House, Senate, gubernatorial, and state legislative races. Meanwhile, the two campaign committees provided
nearly $6 million to Senate candidates and almost $3 million to
House contestants.

The Republican effort went well beyond these direct forms of
support to candidates running under their banner. At least four
programs deserve much more attention than the brief mention
which can be accorded them here. The first is relatively simple.
The RNC provides numerous forms of information and training
for a cadre of campaign professionals who will work for Republican candidates. A communications program passes out information
about many perceived weaknesses in Democratic programs and the
virtues of Republican alternatives. Services like these are not included in the direct assistance noted above, assistance which is
legally limited and must be duly reported to the Federal Election
Commission. To a degree which would be hard to determine,
the programs of assistance to a corps of professional campaigners
work to establish a sense of party presence at least among an elite
stratum of election activists.

The most visible of the programs sponsored by the national
Republican party was its televised advertising campaign which
urged citizens to "Vote Republican for a Change." Rather than
attempting to influence any specific race, these "institutional" ads
were designed to improve the public image of the party as a
whole and to raise pointed criticisms of Democrats in general,
particularly their congressional leadership. David Adamany reports that RNC polls recorded a high level of citizen recall of
these ads which caricatured the speaker of the House. But, apart
from the question of their effectiveness, which would be difficult
to ascertain, the fact of their occurrence is itself remarkable. For
the first time, the technology of mass television advertising has
been brought into service in a major program on behalf of a party
rather than its candidate. The three national party committees
cooperated in sponsoring these ads, funding the over $9 million
they cost.

A third program, conducted by the RNC in concert with the
Reagan-Bush committee, sought to mobilize local party organizations in order to identify favorable voters and stimulate their
turnout. Using everything from edited scripts to videotapes, the
"Commitment '80" program trained field organizers who sub-

sequently recruited and trained volunteers at the precinct level to canvass voters and get them to the polls on election day. The RNC spent about $1 million to get the program started and for legal advice on its execution. The majority of the funds for this program were raised and spent locally under an exemption in the campaign laws adopted in 1979, expressly for the purpose of encouraging grass-roots activity.

While measures of the success of "Commitment '80" are not available, Xandra Kayden found that implementation of the program fell short of its planning and conception. In explaining this failure, she argues that the era of door-to-door campaigning has been overtaken by communications technology and social change. But, whatever the reasons for the shortcomings of this program, the experience of "Commitment '80" should caution us against the easy assumption that the finance laws can quickly accomplish political change. Although the enabling legislation was aimed at stimulating local activity, that did not occur spontaneously. Republican planners felt they had to stimulate local involvement through a planned program and spending from Washington. The amendment, thus, did not overcome the trend toward nationalization which has been changing the balance of political forces in presidential elections. In the 1976 elections, the first conducted under the FECA, local politicians were told by the national party and presidential campaigns not to spend funds which could be assessed against the limits allotted by the law. It may be that one election cycle was required to educate local party leaders that they could now legally raise and spend funds on behalf of the presidential candidate. Therefore, the question of whether or not the law can affect political change in the long run must, for the present, remain unanswered. In the short run, the flow of political money is more likely to reflect the existing array of political power rather than to alter it.

The last RNC program which deserves mention here was an effort to harness the national party expertise and contacts to develop a secure financial base for various state parties; in short, it was an attempt to counter the recent trend of nationalization of money flowing into federal campaigns. Mainly by organizing a series of "unity dinners" attended by the candidates for the party's presidential nomination, an independent staff in Washington was able to raise about $9 million to benefit the Republican parties in a dozen targeted states. According to Kayden, about 35 percent of these funds were spent on "get-out-the-vote" efforts which, of course, aided the national ticket as well as other party nominees. She considers it more noteworthy, however, that the remainder went to overhead for the state parties involved. Through this program, national political forces were used to generate resources for state party organizations; but note that the selection of which states were to be helped was based upon the requirements of the national ticket. From the viewpoint of the national campaigners, furthermore, the fact that such a high percentage went to state party overhead may not have been perceived as optimal, given that their primary purpose was to find a means of getting more money into the presidential election through this exemption in the law.

While the growing organizational strength of the national Republican party has only recently become visible, the roots of these developments can be traced back to the Goldwater defeat. The RNC first began its direct mail program in the 1960s, for example, and for most of this period it led the Democratic party in its efforts to provide information and campaign expertise to its candidates. Taken as a whole, the Republican side of the 1980 elections involved considerable activity and money directed through party channels, a change which runs counter to the complete ascendancy of temporary campaign organizations of the contending candidates which has characterized recent elections. While the RNC was not always successful—for example, an effort to plan well in advance for the Reagan transition was largely ignored by Reagan's advisers—they certainly have demonstrated that Republican party organizations are thriving concerns.

THE NATIONAL DEMOCRATIC PARTY

Institutionally, the Democratic party apparatus in Washington is identical to that of the Republicans: the Democratic National Committee (DNC) serves as the party's highest authority in the four years between nominating conventions, while the Democratic Senatorial Campaign Committee (DSCC) and the Democratic Congressional Campaign Committee (DCCC) work to assist party nominees for those two bodies with money and expertise. The similarity, however, exists only in their formal functions;

performance of Democratic party committees falls well behind that of their opposition. As a result, while the national Democratic party has been vastly more aggressive in asserting its political dominance over its state affiliates in matters such as delegate selection, the influence of the party organizations at all levels of the electoral system has not undergone the same sustained development that we have witnessed in Republican institutions. The disparity between Democrats and Republicans can be traced to four factors: organized labor, incumbency, demographics, and money.

Organized labor has been enormously helpful to Democratic candidates and the Democratic party generally. On the one hand, the political action committees (PACs) formed by labor unions contributed $13.2 million to federal candidates during the 1980 elections, of which about 93 percent went to Democratic candidates. During the same period, labor helped maintain the national party apparatus. The various national party committees received almost $600,000 from labor PACs, most of which went to the DNC. On the other hand, labor unions also provide a ready source of organized volunteers for Democratic candidates and an alternative conduit for reaching and influencing a substantial number of regular party voters. While estimates of the potency of organized labor are extremely difficult to gather, it appears probable that labor committees spent around $15 million advocating the reelection of Carter through "internal communication" costs and "get-out-the-vote" efforts.

All this help has removed much of the incentive for Democrats to develop their party institutions as an essential means of raising and organizing political resources. Labor has, in effect, made it too easy for Democrats.

Incumbency has probably had much the same influence. The national party committees of an incumbent President have historically been closely controlled by the White House. As Frank Sorauf has observed, "So pervasive has the influence of the Presidency been on the national parties that the problem of control can best be divided in two: the situation in the party holding the Presidency and that of the party out of power."

If anything, the Carter administration was less interested in building party institutions than its predecessors. David Adamany quotes party insiders to make two points: first, during most of the

Carter years the best talent and all of the political decision making
was drawn into the White House; and, second, during the 1980
elections the DNC functioned as little more than an arm of the
Carter-Mondale organization. As a result, the party organization
was not systematically cultivated as an *independent force* in electoral politics. It was instead used as a vehicle for Carter's benefit,
even to the point that during the nomination struggle with Kennedy, the DNC and its chair "scarcely maintained even the fiction
of neutrality." Yet, despite these observations, in reflecting upon
his defeat, Carter later referred to the party as "an albatross
around his neck."

Adamany argues that incumbency at the congressional level
has also served to sap the development of a stronger Democratic
party apparatus. The large staffs available to members of the
majority provide many of the services, such as research or public
relations, which might otherwise be developed through party
channels. Incumbents do have less difficulty raising sufficient campaign funds through direct contributions, particularly those from
PACs. Thus, for the party with a majority of both houses, few
incentives existed during the 1960s and 1970s to build up the
party institutions.

The differences in demographics between the two parties may
ultimately affect the ability of the Democrats to raise sums com-
parable to the Republicans. Since the traditional constituencies
of the Democratic party are not generally affluent, direct mail
fund raising may never be as successful for them as it has been for
the Republicans, even though the Democrats currently have a
larger pool of potential supporters. Despite the fact that the
average direct mail contribution is quite small, research on contribution patterns reveals that income is directly and strongly
related to political giving.

Finally, the absence of ample finances is itself a contributing
factor to the inability of the national Democratic party organizations to sponsor the same range of visible programs as the Republicans. While the latter raised approximately $161 million in
1979 and 1980, Democrats raised only around $37 million. Ada-
many reports that this four-to-one ratio was almost duplicated by
the receipts of the state and local party organizations that report
to the FEC. Where Republican committees raised $35 million,
Democrats raised $9 million.

Because of the lack of parity in fund raising, it is not too surprising to find that the help the Democratic party organizations can give to their candidates is correspondingly less (see Table 1). According to the latest figures supplied by the FEC, Republicans led Democrats in support given their candidates by approximately $17 million to $6.6 million. In support of federal candidates alone, around $3.4 million—75 percent of that allowed—was spent by the national party committee on behalf of the Carter-Mondale campaign, while all the national party committees mustered another $2.4 million in contributions to congressional and senatorial candidates or spending on their behalf.

TABLE 1. LEVELS OF PARTY AND PAC SUPPORT IN THE 1980 ELECTIONS
(Thousands of Dollars)

	Democratic	*Republican*	*Total*
National party contributions	$ 1,269	3,747	4,916
State and local contributions	384	781	1,165
National expenditures	4,566	11,607	16,173
State and local expenditures	375	837	1,212
Total party support	$ 6,594	16,972	23,466
Total PAC contributions	$ 28,896	26,222	55,118

In passing, we should note that the figures in Table 1 reveal that even with the massive amounts of support provided by Republican committees, party money falls well below the funds contributed by political action committees. For every dollar the party puts into federal elections, PACs give $2.30. This balance of money is most disadvantageous to parties on the congressional level where they provided $7.6 million and PACs contributed $37.9 million, a ratio of five-to-one. If legislators pay attention to the sources of their campaign money, party interests are severely handicapped in their competition with interest groups.

The general lack of funds on the Democratic side also means that the elaborate series of party programs and services evident at the RNC are nearly absent at the DNC. Inevitably, in the heat of a strongly contested election, expenditures on party programs, such as institutional advertising, will be deemed less useful than direct aid to the candidates running for office, especially when those allocating funds are themselves candidates as in the leader-

ship of the campaign committees on "the Hill." It follows that
the more indirect forms of party help will be given substantial
funding only after the foundation of direct contributions and
expenditures has been securely built.

Nevertheless, the Democrats have developed some new programs such as PAC briefings and training conferences. In the heat
of recent election fights both parties have taken on an additional
function of "cueing" PAC giving. By holding periodic briefings
for PAC representatives in which the progress of key House and
Senate races could be closely reviewed, party operatives attempt
to direct PAC contributions into winnable races. And for the 1982
elections, the Democrats also imitated the Republican lead by
stepping up their seminars to exchange technical expertise for
campaign managers and by sponsoring the first "Issue Training
Conference" for their candidates to learn criticisms of Reagan's
programs and new ideas for Democratic alternatives. While the
differences are still major, it appears fair to observe that at least
the seeds of Democratic growth became evident during the early
Reagan years. Yet, whether they would flower remained very
much a question.

Table 2 contains the raw figures of how the campaign committees allocated their funds. They appear to show a substantial tilt
toward incumbents by the Democratic campaign committees,
leading to the conclusion that incumbents have used their campaign committees to concentrate resources on themselves. However, the party comparisons in Table 2 overstate this inequity to
a substantial degree, since more Democratic incumbents were running for reelection. When the total amounts provided to candidates are averaged, the results are quite different. In Table 3, one
discovers that both parties used what resources they had to aid
incumbents (with opposition) and open-seat contestants. In November 1980, incumbents ran for reelection in all but forty-three
districts. The Democrats put about 25 percent of their effort into
thirty-seven of those open contests, mostly as contributions to
the candidates. As a result, they received, on average, about $3,500
from the party.

Republicans also provided greater support to open-seat competitors, while the average challenger of an incumbent Democrat
was, comparatively, left to find other sources of money. One
interesting difference is that while the RNCC *gave* money to their

TABLE 2.   DISTRIBUTION OF SUPPORT BY PARTY CAMPAIGN COMMITTEES TO
CATEGORIES OF CANDIDACY IN 1980

	Total Dollars (000's)	Incumbent %	Challenger %	Open Seat %
A. SENATE CANDIDATES				
Democrats				
Contributions	$ 482	61	26	13
Spending	589	62	30	8
Total support	$ 1,071	62	28	10
Republicans				
Contributions	$ 415	27	55	18
Spending	5,026	9	66	25
Total support	$ 5,441	10	65	24
B. HOUSE CANDIDATES				
Democrats				
Contributions	$ 614	55	21	24
Spending	35	17	55	28
Total support	$ 649	53	23	24
Republicans				
Contributions	$ 2,003	55	31	15
Spending	1,229	18	54	28
Total support	$ 3,232	41	40	20

TABLE 3.   AVERAGE LEVEL OF SUPPORT BY HOUSE CAMPAIGN COMMITTEES BY
CATEGORY OF CANDIDACY, 1980

	Incumbent	Challenger	Open Seat
A. Contributions to Candidates (in dollars)			
Democrats	$ 1,476	935	3,419
Republicans	$ 7,986	2,712	6,977
B. Spending on Behalf of Candidates (in dollars)			
Democrats	$ 26	138	233
Republicans	$ 1,601	2,900	8,000

incumbents, they tended to *spend* the available money for their nonincumbents. Perhaps they felt the incumbents had greater experience in how to conduct their own campaigns; perhaps their incumbents wanted their money under their own control.

Table 4 contains the equivalent figures for party support of Senate candidates. The data are slightly more complex since

TABLE 4. AVERAGE AMOUNT OF SUPPORT BY SENATE CAMPAIGN COMMITTEES
BY CATEGORY OF CANDIDACY, 1980

	Incumbent	Challenger	Open Seat
A. *Contributions to Candidates* (in thousands of dollars)			
Democrats	$ 16.3	20.8	7.0
Republicans	$ 12.4	12.7	8.3
B. *Spending on Behalf of Candidates* (in cents per voter)			
Democrats	0.63	1.84	0.11
Republicans	3.13	5.72	2.86

spending figures must be related to the size of the state. (In calculating Part B, the average amount spent on each senator was divided by the average size of the state for the category of candidate. Thus, when the detailed records of each candidate are released by the FEC, these figures may change slightly.) In both parties, candidates challenging incumbents received a greater average level of support from their campaign committees than did even the incumbents. And, in Senate races, it was the open-seat competitors who were allowed to fend for themselves by their party.

Taken as a whole, these data do not suggest an overwhelming proincumbent bias in the passing out of party money. The evidence indicates that both parties are using strategically whatever funds they do have; that is to say, they appear to be putting the money into the most competitive races. The disparities are even larger than they appear in Tables 3 and 4, since these figures are average contributions, and the parties do not support all candidates within a given category. For example, among Democratic candidates for the House, the party contributed funds to 86 percent of the open-seat contestants, but to only 36 percent of the incumbents running and to 28 percent of the challengers. Moreover, since incumbents are the most likely to win (even with the higher turnover rate in recent Senate contests), it seems only logical that they would receive important support from their party's campaign committee.

The finding that both party campaign committees invest their money strategically, rather than use it to relieve incumbents from the burdens of fund raising, could be very important when considering changes that might be made in the law. If the limitations on what parties could contribute and spend were responsible for a wider distribution of resources beyond protecting incumbents, then one might be less willing to eliminate these party limits. However, it appears to the contrary that the campaign committees are not "maxing out" on incumbents and only then taking care of everyone else.

In the aftermath of the 1980 elections, the greatest unknown is whether the Democrats will be able to replicate the RNC successes and place their party committees in a more secure financial position. Given the time-lag and the initial investment costs necessary to build a direct mail program, they are now at a considerable disadvantage; though a compensatory factor may be the opportunity to learn from the RNC mistakes and successes. At issue is whether we will have stronger American parties or merely better funded Republican party organizations.

American journalists and political scientists have normally assumed that symmetry would prevail in the organizational design of the two major parties. The pressures toward coalitional, pragmatic parties, to adopt Orren's phrasing, have forced party leaders to adopt similar techniques of organization. What has proved successful for one party will—we assume with a good deal of historical support—quickly be imitated by the other.

European scholars, on the other hand, usually do not assume that political parties will naturally resemble each other structurally. As Maurice Duverger argues, the requirements of reaching out to different classes and constituencies inevitably impose distinctive patterns of organization. Socialist parties, for example, will exhibit very dissimilar characteristics from those appealing to an upper middle-class clientele.

The point of introducing this argument into the discussion is not, however, to propose that American parties are necessarily evolving toward the structural differences found in European examples. Rather, I intend simply to add a cautionary note to what has been mostly an unquestioned assumption in American thinking about parties. In the recent past our two parties have been changing as a consequence of the unique political tensions. While the national Democratic party has been more assertive in infringing the prerogative and powers of its state level affiliates upon matters of delegate selection, change in the Republican party has been driven by its fund-raising strategy in response to the party's minority status. The assumption that inevitably the parties will converge to reestablish symmetrical organizations must be advanced with due skepticism; certainly it cannot be offered as proof that the Democratic party will naturally replicate the Republican success.

Parties and the Federal Election Campaign Act

Any complete assessment of the impact of the national campaign finance legislation upon political parties must inevitably come to a mixed conclusion. To the degree that the law does affect the capabilities of party organizations, in some respects the law facilitates party activity, while other provisions advantage different electoral institutions that are, in a sense, competitive with parties. At the same time, it is almost certainly the case that the campaign laws are but a minor element in the overall constellation of forces that are weakening or strengthening party institutions.

Given the complexity of how money is raised and spent in electoral politics evident in Table 5, it is easy to see how the campaign laws could simultaneously benefit and handicap political parties.

Party scholars who believe that the finance laws are detrimental to political parties raise some strong arguments to support their position. Where the law provides public funding in the presidential race, the money goes directly to the candidates rather than through the party committees. The act also limits parties in what they can spend on behalf of their candidates, while wealthy individuals and political action committees are able to spend unlimited amounts on independent expenditures. While the act does not directly encourage the growth of political action committees, it has provided the environment in which contributions by PACs are increasingly important in the receipts of congressional and senatorial candidates. Finally, the law restricts campaign budgets, either through the limitations on spending by presidential candidates or through sharply circumscribed contribution limits for all federal candidates. Since there is some evidence to support the contention of campaign managers that meager resources force them to rely more heavily upon the mass media, the act may have indirectly undercut the volunteer, person-to-person activities that have traditionally been the strength of party committees.

TABLE 5. TEN WAYS OF SPENDING CAMPAIGN MONEY IN FEDERAL ELECTIONS

1. *Campaign Treasuries of Presidential Candidates*
Public funding is provided directly to presidential candidates in both the prenomination and general election races. In return, the expenditures of the candidates are strictly limited.

2. *Compliance Funds*
Presidential candidates can raise and spend additional funds for costs of complying with the laws. While theoretically unlimited in amount, the expenditures from this account are subject to FEC audit to determine their appropriateness.

3. *National Party Conventions*
The national nominating conventions of major parties are financed out of the public treasury and strictly limited in the total that can be expended. Clearly this category of spending benefits the party, the presidential candidates, and other party officeholders.

4. *National Party Spending Directly Associated with the Presidential Campaign*
A limited amount of funds can be raised from private sources by the national party committees. In both major parties, these funds are entirely controlled by the candidate committee; they are treated as merely a separate bank account.

5. *Party Money for Congressional and Senatorial Candidates*
Party committees may expend money on behalf of their candidates for federal office. *One* of the national committees *and* the state party can each spend $10,000 for a congressional candidate, and two cents per voting-age citizen or $20,000 (whichever is larger) for a senatorial candidate. These amounts are increased by cost-of-living adjustments since the act was passed; so the limitation for congressional candidates in 1980 was $14,700 (i.e., a total of $29,400), while spending for senators varied from a high of $485,024 (California) to the minimum of $29,400. These allot-

ments can be doubled if both the state party and the national committee
are spending on the candidate's behalf.

In addition, *either* the national party committee or the campaign
committee may *contribute* $17,500 to senatorial candidates in either the
primary or general election; while both committees can each contribute
$5,000 to a congressional candidate in both the primary and general elec-
tions (i.e., $20,000 total). Finally, the state party committees may con-
tribute $5,000 to Senate and House candidates in both types of elections,
as can any local party committee that can prove it is independent of its
state committee.

6. National Committee Operating Budgets
The normal operation of the national parties can be funded quite separately and is essentially unlimited as long as it does not involve the express advocacy of the defeat or election of a specific candidate. Under this
provision, the Republicans sponsored the "Vote Republican for a
Change" ads.

7. Grass-roots Activity of Local Party Committees
An exemption was included in the act in 1979 for certain classes of party
spending for citizen-to-citizen contact and "get-out-the-vote" activities.
In addition, local party committees which raise and spend under $5,000
can avoid the reporting requirements of the FECA.

8. State Party Money
State law may regulate the contributions and expenditures to state
parties, but these are only affected by the federal law when these committees are involved in federal elections. During a presidential election,
these funds, referred to as "soft money," can be mixed with the legally
limited federal money in proportion to the number of candidates on the
ballot in a given location, thereby allowing campaigners to spend more
for ticket-wide activities.

9. Labor Union, Trade Association, and Corporation Money
These organizations can spend funds for "get-out-the-vote" efforts or
"internal communications" to their membership without reporting these
expenditures under the act.

10. Independent Expenditures
Individuals and groups can spend unlimited amounts advocating the defeat or election of federal candidates as long as the expenditures are
independent of the candidate, that is, not made in consultation or
coordination with the candidate or his or her representatives.

Of all these effects, the most detrimental aspects of the law for
political parties come about through the advantages open to institutional competitors. For example, over the past five elections,
congressional candidates have become increasingly dependent
upon funds channeled through political action committees (see

Table 6). At the governing stage, they are real competitors to
parties for influence upon the behavior of public officeholders.
Most PAC officials look upon contributions as a component of
their lobbying strategy. Money facilitates at least access. Another
major problem for parties is the growing level of independent
expenditures. Because of the Supreme Court's landmark ruling
in *Buckley v. Valeo,* this spending is not limited by law, while the
support that parties can give to their candidates has strict ceilings. Designing an effective policy response to counter these two
developments will be extremely difficult, since the latter is constitutionally protected, while an attempt to limit PAC giving will
most likely direct money into even greater levels of independent
expenditures.

On the other hand, the FECA does contain numerous provisions
which are generally beneficial to political party committees. First,
the law allows individuals to contribute $20,000 to political par-
ties where they are only able to give $1,000 to candidates or
PACs.

As the detailed information in Table 5 makes clear, party committees are also given favored status in aiding candidates for
federal office. They are allowed higher limits for contributions to

TABLE 6. SOURCES OF CONTRIBUTIONS TO HOUSE CANDIDATES BY PARTY,
1972–1980

	1972	1974	1976	1978	1980 *
Republicans					
Individuals	62	76	62	63	66
Political parties	23	7	12	7	9
Nonparty committees	9	12	18	23	25
Candidates	—	4	6	7	—**
Democrats					
Individuals	56	70	55	60	66
Political parties	12	1	4	2	2
Nonparty committees	19	22	28	27	32
Candidates	—	7	11	11	—**

Source: Jacobson, Gary C., "The Pattern of Campaign Contributions to Candidates for the U.S. House of Representatives, 1972–78," *An Analysis of the Impact
of the Federal Election Campaign Act, 1972–78,* A Report to the Committee on
House Administration, U.S. House of Representatives, October 1979.

* FEC data   ** Included in "Individuals"

their candidates than are nonparty committees, and parties are entitled to spend additional sums in "consultation or coordination" with candidates running for federal offices under their banner. For example, each party could expend $4.6 million on behalf of its presidential candidates. For legislative candidates, the law makes separate provision for support by the national and state parties. The Republicans, however, have set up a series of "'agency agreements" in which both the RNC and the state parties designate the relevant national campaign committee as their agent, so that party spending can be a concerted effort and, they hope, a more potent factor.

Under another provision of the campaign laws, local and state parties are allowed unlimited spending on behalf of their presidential candidates for specifically exempted campaign activities such as "get-out-the-vote" or other types of traditional efforts involving volunteers. Furthermore, if the receipts and expenditures of party committees are below $5,000, they are exempted from the federal reporting requirements. According to the Campaign Finance Study Group of the Institute of Politics at Harvard University, the vast majority of party committees organized on the local level fall well short of this threshold.

All of these provisions add up to something of a favored status for parties under the finance laws. Whether these provisions do enough to reinforce the political power of parties or whether additional changes would be desirable are debatable points, discussed in more detail later. One can argue, for example, that party committees traditionally raised and spent *all* of the election money on behalf of their candidates, and now they are reduced to a percentage. But that situation developed before the act was passed; the laws merely acknowledged the existing financial independence of candidates.

Among the most beneficial provisions of the current law, probably the most important are those which allow greater contributions to party committees and permit party spending on behalf of candidates. But these provisions are in and of themselves less important than their effects, given the total architecture of the act. Specifically, the sections of the law which attempt to limit the flow of money into and from *candidate* treasuries have established the circumstances in which political professionals now strive to increase *party* money. The contribution limits, for example, have made campaign funds extremely difficult to raise, so candidates now turn to their party committees for help. On the presidential level, expenditure limitations increase the incentive for politicians to explore state and local party institutions as mechanisms for getting more money into the campaign. At present, these provisions are under attack and suggestions abound for ways of allowing greater money to go to candidates. While such moves may be justifiable on their own merits, they will have the effect of diminishing incentives for directing money through parties.

Even within the provisions regulating party money, we may find that the current limitations have some useful by-products. For example, the ceilings on what parties may do in direct support of their candidates are at least partially responsible for the willingness of the RNC to spend large sums on less direct forms of election advocacy such as the party advertisements, helping state parties, or even their 1981 efforts to help state legislators draw new congressional and legislative districts.

The Impact of Finance Laws

In assessing the consequences of the campaign finance legislation, therefore, it is not sufficient to weigh only those provisions directly beneficial or detrimental to political parties. Especially in considering desired policy changes, one must bring into the analysis the total fabric of the act as it shapes the flow of political money through candidate treasuries, PACs, and parties. The effects are clearly mixed. Parties are handicapped in fulfilling traditional functions by some aspects of the law, even while they enjoy some advantages denied other electoral institutions.

Moreover, in examining the details of the campaign act, we must not lose sight of the fact that these laws are not solely responsible for the resurgence of the Republican party organizations. The computer technology so necessary for raising money through mass mailings is at least as important, and probably would have been pressed into service with equal success even in the absence of the act. The RNC began its direct mail program in the 1960s. As permanent organizations, parties may well be better able to undertake the long lead time necessary to develop direct mail lists than are temporary candidate campaigns. And, given adequate resources, there is nothing so striking in the contemporary communications mix about a party attacking its opponent in a national television advertising campaign. Finally, the pressure toward nationalization of political forces can also be seen as a more general phenomenon caused by deeper forces. In this sense, what has happened to parties is but one aspect of a broad development; the growth of political action committees is another. In presidential politics, we observe recent Supreme Court decisions which give the national parties supremacy over the selection of national convention delegates. And, in congressional politics, the rise of incumbency and the decline of marginal districts are other manifestations of this national trend.

Finally, we should bear in mind an important point raised earlier: the finance laws cannot alter the fundamental arrangements of power among electoral institutions, at least in the short run. For example, in keeping with the 1979 amendments, local and state party committees spent about $12 million on grassroots campaign activities (75 percent of this by Republican committees). When asked about their experiences in raising and spending this money, however, many state party officials, particularly on the Democratic side, candidly admit that much of it was done by national political operatives using the local party bank accounts as a convenient cover. And, as noted above, the Republican Commitment '80 program originated as a national effort to stimulate local activity. Whether these patterns will be repeated as local party organizations learn what they can legally do under the act will be an important matter to observe in future elections. At least the first time through with this provision in place, the results were not as local, not as grass-roots, and not as spontaneous as envisioned.

Party Renewal or Political Change?

Summing up the argument to this point, we have observed that, at least on the Republican side, party activity at the national level is on the upswing and that party money is becoming an increasingly important aspect of the campaigns mobilized by Republican candidates. The evidence is, however, ambiguous, for the Democrats have fallen far short of their opponents. While we hear firm pledges from Washington of their determination to catch up, we cannot be sure Democrats will succeed in the near future. In any case, this resurgence cannot be wholly attributed to the recent campaign finance legislation, which has had beneficial as well as detrimental consequences for parties, and which is but one causal factor—and perhaps a weak one—in a complex set of political, social, and technological changes.

As the next logical step in this analysis, we should examine whether this growing party strength constitutes a renewal of our traditional notions of parties or a new development. On this score, the available evidence is quite persuasive that these recent trends portend a different basis of power for party committees than has been their primary source of political influence in the past.

As noted at the outset, one important change is the increasing potency of national parties, which have never had a very pronounced role in the election of candidates even for federal office. Perhaps an even more significant change, however, is based upon the recognition that while party committees may be strengthened organizationally, an entirely separate question is whether or not they are becoming stronger *politically*. Concern with the role of parties in governance directs attention directly toward the political strength of parties rather than their ability to raise and spend substantial sums.

The nationalization point seems pretty straightforward. Historically, national parties have not had much of an independent existence. They did not contribute substantial sums to congressional or senatorial campaigns. Where party money was an important component of campaign war chests, it was channeled through the state or local committee. Where national committees were little more than confederations of state parties, they now have an independent existence. They raise and spend substantial sums on their own operations; they have ongoing programs of gathering information useful to their candidates and providing training and consultation in election techniques; they produce and distribute news spots for radio and television stations; and, as the data above indicate, they are growing in importance as a conduit for campaign money. Now the national committees are reaching out to help their state affiliates in a complete reversal of roles. Programs at the RNC include reinforcing state parties, aiding in the recruitment and support of even state legislative candidates, and providing technical assistance (to the tune of

$1.5 million) to Republicans in battles over congressional and state legislative redistricting.

The intriguing question in all this organizational development is whether that power will reach backwards to bring party influence more forcefully to bear upon national legislative politics. In broad sweeps, the scholarship on congressional behavior provides some hope that this linkage will occur. Political scientists David R. Mayhew and Richard Fenno argue that the dynamics of electoral politics directly invest the functioning of the Congress, in everything from floor votes to speeches to committee work to sponsorship of legislation and so on. But they also argue that, at present, individual survival is the most powerful incentive at work; that is, collective *party* survival has not been a very prominent factor in recent years.

These incentives could, perhaps, be altered by manipulating the mix of available financial resources through the campaign laws, manufacturing a scarcity of nonparty funds while reinforcing the privileged position of parties. The major stumbling block to accomplishing this task is, of course, the fact that the legislature writes the finance rules.

While we cannot predict whether the campaign purse strings controlled by parties will ever be used to influence congressional behavior, we can start by examining whether financial strength gives parties a different basis of political muscle than has traditionally been true. To do so, however, requires that we focus upon models of party functioning at the state level, since we have no experience with strong party committees at the national level.

Theoretically, a major governmental function of political parties is to generate a degree of consensus on policy matters among political leadership. Elected officials serving at different levels and in different branches of government and who share a common party background presumably have similar views about the major direction of public policy. Party politics in the legislative arena, furthermore, serve to reduce the number of policy options which can be considered politically viable. The mechanisms of majority parties for achieving consensus on policy options are said to produce, in the process, a wide range of harmonized interests. That is, parties are coalition-building mechanisms both in terms of generating agreement among interests and in harnessing pressures to incorporate in the bargaining the widest possible set of interests.

Certainly American political parties have frequently fallen short of this ideal model; nevertheless, parties have generally provided pressure upon public officials toward consensus and coalition-building and away from the particularism of regional, ethnic, sectarian, or interest-group politics. How have they traditionally mobilized this pressure?

Control over party recruitment by a single party leader, for example, is one mechanism through which the party influence upon politicians has been instituted. Although complete control has been rare on a state-wide level, more common have been instances in urban political machines in which a single individual, whether a public official or not, has dominated party nominations across the whole range of public offices. As a result, this individual has, presumably, exercised as well considerable influence over governmental decision making, thereby bridging the separation of powers by selecting nominees with harmonious policy views and keeping them working together once they hold office.

I suspect, however, that strong party leaders were never as dictatorial as they appear to have been in our folklore, particularly on the state level. A careful study of Connecticut Democratic boss John Bailey, for example, reveals that he rarely reached a major decision without a considerable amount of consultation with lesser party figures. Bailey could control the timing, nature, and extent of these consultations; he was clearly first among equals. But, he did not simply give orders; his power was based upon maintaining satisfied subordinates.

A more decentralized variant of this power is found in party nominating procedures which forced recruitment to many levels of the political system through the same institution, usually the local party committee. These committees would send delegates to different conventions at which candidates for legislative seats or congressional races or state-wide offices would be nominated. Presumably, those solidly in control of a local party committee sent delegates to the different conventions who would support candidates of similar views. As a result, party institutions worked in the direction of, but certainly could not guarantee, policy consensus.

Applying this basis of party power to the contemporary national scene is, however, a fanciful undertaking. The notion of a small set of party leaders controlling nominations for House and Senate is too far removed from the present realities to be seriously contemplated. Federalism and state legislative authority over party nominations in the states are not going to yield to national party control. We must assume that congressional and senatorial nominations will remain essentially federalized and most likely will be accomplished through primaries rather than caucuses and conventions.

Moreover, we encounter another problem which sharply circumscribes the applicability of the traditional party model to the contemporary problem of governing, even granted strong national parties. When they existed, strong party institutions were rarely organized on the basis of policy concerns; rather they were rooted in matters of patronage and faction. As Frank Sorauf has succinctly observed, "The electoral politics at which the party succeeded was not ideological or issue-centered politics. The parties sought governmental power for patronage and favors more than for the enactment of a party program into law."

In order to achieve these goals, party leaders preferred candidates not from consideration of their policy views but upon estimates of their likelihood of electoral success. This same calculus is, of course, at work in the decisions as to which candidates should receive party support; but here we confront an important distinction between the campaign politics of the present and those which were dominated by strong party institutions. The "science" of predicting electoral success fifty years ago was very different from our present methods. For one thing, estimates of which personalities and programs would appeal to the rank and file must have been a good deal cruder before polling technology developed. Most likely, the process and standards by which acceptability was tested by party leaders resembled the methods used today by members of Congress to gauge how opinion in their districts is changing, i.e., through reliance upon established networks of politically active sub-elites. In fact, voter opinion may have mattered a good deal less than whether or not local party cadres could be mobilized to work for a given candidacy.

Much has changed. The possibilities of testing citizen opinion and predicting voter behavior have improved markedly. Communications technology now allows candidates to reach potential voters directly without requiring a decentralized, personalized, and enduring party structure. As government itself has grown in scope and authority, not only has it assumed many of the patronage functions, but also the stakes of election contests have become a good deal more consequential, and the policy component of the electoral process has become a good deal more salient.

These broad changes in the manner of constructing political support direct our attention not to the relationship between party leaders and public officeholders, but rather toward the connections between elected officials and voters. Accepting the fact that politics has become a good deal more plebiscitarian in nature, what functions have parties traditionally fulfilled in this domain? Can these be strengthened by a resurgence of party finances?

First, parties symbolize an effective tie among groups of voters and between voters and a policy tradition. Party nominations are still valuable to politicians, in part, because they cognitively link their candidacies to a history of rewards and benefits and a tradition of group and self-identifications. If like-minded and knowledgeable citizens form into cohesive coalitions and vote consistently across a range of elective offices, then the problems of governance are eased considerably.

This linkage is the basis of party alignments and realignments about which political scientist Walter Dean Burnham and others have written so extensively. And, while this is not the proper forum for an extended discussion of whether or not alignment politics at the voter level have broken down, we can at least follow James Sundquist's lead in recognizing that the construction and maintenance of an electoral coalition is the result of an interactive process between party leadership and currents of citizen opinion.

If anything, technological change ought to have facilitated that interaction. Voters learn more direct information now about candidates as the latter communicate their campaign themes to gain visibility and support, and candidates know much more precisely what voters are thinking. As a result, it may be that the interaction is now *too* sensitive. Voters are exposed to the differences among politicians of the same party, and candidates can alter their messages as popular opinion shifts outside of traditional party contours. Politics may now lack an inertia which formerly characterized the dynamics of coalition decline and realignment, inertia through which political elites at times became progressively out of step with their electoral constituencies to the point that old coalitions splintered and reformed.

Given this argument, the prospects for stronger national parties recasting the electoral coalitions do not appear to be great. We can still hope that those staffing the party apparatus will be able to articulate and communicate to voters less transient messages to the extent they gain some independence from their own office-holders. In this regard, the recent Republican experience is not the most auspicious start imaginable. For one thing, the direct mail program tends to compartmentalize party supporters according to the appeals to which they respond—the party has its lists of those who give on the basis of social issues, economic conservatism, the Panama Canal, etc. It is as if contributors were members of different parties rather than a single roster. The party advertising program in 1979 and 1980, moreover, was largely an attack upon the opposition, not a presentation of alternative policies. Reportedly, these ads will be replicated in 1982 under the slogan "Leadership that Works for a Change," but as of this writing it remains uncertain whether the new ads will portray differences in party policy or will merely emphasize "leadership." In any case, to the extent that party advertisements are able to revitalize a *sense* of party difference, they will be a facilitating factor in governance. (Certainly President Reagan's dedication to changing the direction of governmental policy is vastly more important in transmitting an awareness that partisan differences do matter.)

It appears, therefore, that the most we can hope for on the citizen end of the relationship between candidates and voters is that parties will provide pressure to ease the problems of governance. On the other side of this interaction, however, stronger party committees can also have some influence over the messages their candidates deliver. The RNC, for example, regularly sends out material to counter Democratic attacks upon Reagan's programs. "Most of our communications effort here is aimed at generating support for presidential programs, rather than electing candidates," revealed one party official with whom I discussed this matter. He went on to note that by training a band of campaign managers and press secretaries, the committee's message might "infiltrate" the political discourse of Republican candidates. If these candidates became publicly committed to supporting the President's programs during the election, they would be more loyal once in office.

Ultimately, however, the party's ability to provide needed resources to its candidates should be its most powerful weapon. But, can it use that weapon? Does the national Republican party get anything for all those contributions, all those expenditures, and all the expertise it makes available?

Historically, political parties have provided essential services to their candidates. The need for election resources was, in fact, the primary reason why party committees were first organized. These organizations were not useful to politicians because they generated a policy consensus among elites or built coalitions of interest groups or forced them to bargain in the process of winning elections. If these things occurred, they were the happy by-products of the real utility of parties; they were fundamentally a technology of constructing electoral support. The structure of block and precinct captains and ward and city bosses was a necessary means of communicating with voters. In the absence of the mass media and polling, politicians needed the party structure for its services, much as they require financial and technological assistance under the present circumstances.

There is, however, a difference. The party structure had the capacity to choose among candidates and to deny services to politicians, presumably because personnel embedded in the organization would not work for a given candidate. The question to be addressed, therefore, is what flexibility does the national Republican party exercise over providing resources to candidates.

In 1980, national Republican money was not distributed evenly to all candidates. Funds were allocated on a triage basis: safe incumbents and the most marginal challengers were given less (often nothing), while candidates running where ample funds might make a real difference received party support. In campaign jargon, candidates were "targeted."

The party could, therefore, choose among candidates. Nevertheless, decision making was not based upon the policy positions of the candidates; as in the grand old days, estimates of electability dominated the party choice. According to the RNC's counsel, Mark Braden, neither ideology nor issues entered into decisions of which candidates should receive the maximum support. Since they did not allocate their funds upon willingness to commit the candidacy to policy positions, the party committees have had less influence on the behavior of successful recipients once they took office.

"Electability" is, of course, the standard for party recruitment under the traditional party model. When it came to governing, however, centralized control by party leaders compensated for the absence of a policy component during the electoral stage. But centralized direction on the national level is absent and not likely to develop.

Recently, the RNC has also been involved in candidate recruitment. Twenty regional political directors encourage candidates to run, while discouraging others. At times, their efforts even extend down to the level of state legislative candidates. Here again, however, the party preference among potential candidates is basically determined by prediction of which candidate has the best potential for victory in the general election; at least that is the way recruitment works in theory. "We operate on the premise," one RNC official told me, "that we represent the Republican party, not a particular faction of the Republican party." He went on to imply, however, that he was speaking about official party policy and that sometimes the regional director might allow policy views to enter into their calculations of electability.

How successful their discouragement is remains unclear. On the one hand, if the party believes that a candidacy is hopeless, that candidate is not likely to receive substantial support in the general election. Yet, on the other hand, both sets of national party committees have been reluctant to enter primary contests once they were joined. In the few instances in which the RNC did actively support one primary candidate over another—Minnesota's gubernatorial race and Iowa's senatorial contest—the supported candidate lost. Of course, that sort of defeat for the party used to happen with some regularity when "reformers" ran against and beat the party machine. But now the consequences of backing primary candidates appear to be very distasteful to party decision makers.

Finally, the finances of the national party machinery were used during the legislative fights of 1981 to bolster support for Reagan tax and budget cuts. Elaborate plans were laid for a program to stimulate pressure upon Congress from both organized groups (such as chambers of commerce) and individual citizens. The actual achievements, however, did not live up to expectations. "The program never quite got into place; we did only about half of what we'd conceived."

Much of this effort was directed at potential votes from Democratic members of Congress, rather than at reinforcing their own party's leadership. Nevertheless, the use of party machinery and finances to mobilize citizen opinion has provocative potential. Carried to an extreme, party committees might use this citizen link to pressure officeholders into greater party discipline.

In summary, the national party machinery on the Republican side resembles more the functioning of a political action committee than it does a revitalized and nationalized version of traditional parties. Taking advantage of the favorable aspects of the campaign finance laws, they are able to raise significant amounts of money, out of which a substantial percentage is used to maintain the organization itself. Amply funded research provides the basis for targeting election districts and candidates that are "winnable," and funds, advice, expertise, and coordinated spending are directed where the party staff believes they will do most good. The party does not nominate candidates in the sense of selecting them, but it does encourage strong candidates and tries to discourage competitors who might lose. And the party's resources are being used to exert citizen pressure upon Congress, a tactic long employed by interest groups. All of these activities mimic those of PACs.

We have really been discussing two dimensions of nomination politics which can now be stated more explicitly—the problem of control and the basis of choice. Figure 1 displays the logical combinations of these dimensions simplified into dichotomous choices. Much as political scientists may have yearned to change the old parties into "responsible" policy-oriented parties, during the past three decades, nomination politics have become candidate-centered. The driving force behind this trend has not

Fig. 1. Ideal Models of Party Nominations

		CONTROL OVER NOMINATIONS	
		Centralized	Plebiscitarian
BASIS OF SUPPORT	Policy Views	Responsible Parties	Parties as PACs
	Electability	Grand Old Parties	Candidate-Centered Politics

been changes in party rules, but rather social, economic, and technological change over the past eighty years. The question then becomes whether we can force parties back into the bottom left hand quadrant or promote a new conception of the powers, structure, and functioning of parties. The latter I will refer to as the "PAC model" of parties.

Even while troubled somewhat by the "parties as PACs" analogy, I will pursue the discussion here under this rubric primarily because it illuminates the differences from other conceptions of how parties might function.

Specifically, the model toward which parties might evolve resembles little the ideological, "responsible" party organization. Unified, principled parties which could exact ideological purity from their officeholders have proven unattainable in the American political system, despite advocacy by a lineage of political scientists from Woodrow Wilson to E. E. Schattschneider, which culminated in the issuance of a report in 1950 by the American Political Science Association itself. Responsible parties inherently demand centralized leadership capable of disciplining officeholders who break party ranks. Moreover, the model assumes that public policy preferences can be integrated into a logically consistent array of choices rationally deduced from some high-order political values or philosophical principles for government. Elsewhere in this volume, Gary Orren correctly brings to light criticisms of the dangers of ideological politics as tending toward moralism and rigidity which can frustrate the degree of compromise necessary to operate our purposefully fragmented governmental machinery. As Orren concludes, "Responsible parties are neither feasible nor particularly desirable in the United States."

If party organizations were to become more relevant institutions in the discussion and adoption of public policy, in practice they could only do so in forms compatible with our governmental institutions and the communication capacities made available to politicians by current technology. The requirements of what I call here the PAC model for party committees fall far short of the demands made upon responsible parties, both in terms of their capacity to enforce party discipline and the promulgation of a logically consistent ideology.

On the dimension of control, I am led to consider this alternative because I do not believe we will be able to return to domination of nomination politics by party leaders. But to look for other instruments of party influence beyond control over nominations is far from embracing an "antiparty" position, for my view of parties rests upon the desirability of these institutions in preference to candidate-centered politics or single-issue/special interest organizations.

As to the basis upon which party organizations can exert their influence, the "parties as PACs" model does not imply a rigid party doctrine or ideology. Rather, I have in mind the possibility that party institutions could become the arenas within which specific policy proposals could be discussed and debated; they should become more than mere vessels in which the fermentation of competing candidacies and interests takes place. While I do not have a precise sense of the institution which might house this discussion, it may suffice merely to encourage more elaborate and sustained attention to policy matters under the aegis of party committees. I would hope that the party caucuses could be strengthened, that more issue training seminars for party candidates would be held, and that tighter cooperation could be developed between these caucuses and the party committees and the partys' national committees. While I would not expect party discipline—as in the denial of party money to those who broke ranks—to be rigorously enforced except, perhaps, in cases of near unanimity, I would hope that party resources would be used to lobby officeholders to support the party leadership. This lobbying might include both direct pressure from party officials and efforts to mobilize pressure from local party membership. Finally, it may be that the policy adopting machinery of the party, that is, the drafting of quadrennial platforms, will have to be thoroughly revised, as the Democrat's Commission on Party Accountability is currently considering.

In that our politics has become candidate-centered in election and interest group-dominated in legislation, we need to promote institutions which will foster broader coalitions across a range of constituencies in the organized and unorganized public, and institutions which provide greater integration for a fragmented issue agenda by embracing a more expansive range of policy questions. Political action committees have become engines of considerable political energy: they mobilize substantial sums of money, and they coordinate contributions with a sustained lobby-

ing effort. As such, they force the governmental apparatus to
consider policy in very narrow ranges and compartmentalized
arenas. Party organizations, on the other hand, offer the only
prospects for instituting pressures toward addressing a larger
scope of policy matters. They should serve to coalesce PAC and
other group interests.

To be sure, in some cases the party position will be heavily
influenced by "single-interest" or "special interest" groups. But
parties have responsibilities that cut across levels of offices and
parochial geographical constituencies, and they are inevitably
interested in promoting election majorities. In other words, parties differ markedly from PACs in that they are inherently
pluralistic whereas most PACs remain centralized and monolithic.
Major party organizations, therefore, provide pressure toward
greater integration of policy options and broader coalitions. They
offer better mechanisms for policy compromise and coalition
building than does interest groups' lobbying.

What has been missing in our political institutions has been
any need to direct policy discussions through party channels.
Yet, if increasing financial resources can be directed through
parties, they may be able to afford their officeholders some protection from what might be termed "PAC discipline." That protection may be manifest both in terms of counterpressure in
lobbying and in the availability of adequate campaign financing
for those who wish to resist dependency upon PACs. At the same
time, by promoting greater visibility of policy matters through
party activities, elected officials will necessarily become more col-
lectively responsible for governing outcomes.

Strengthening Parties through the Law

In essence, the long-term role change for party committees
involves the loss of control over the awarding of nominations.
Party functionaries used to sit athwart the processes by which information was exchanged between office seekers and voters, and
they used that position to dominate the selection of candidates.
Their roles as brokers and mediators, coalition and consensus
builders, grew out of that power. But they have lost it. They have
lost it not so much to changes in election and party laws, to the
rules of the game, but to the major social, economic, and techno-

logical transformations of the 20th century. Some would have us attempt to squeeze party leaders back into position as mediators between voters and candidates by tinkering with those rules, an effort which minimizes the more profound, underlying changes and ignores the fact that those rule changes must be adopted by officeholders whose power will be thereby curtailed.

Today the prospects for stronger party committees lie not in recapturing that pivotal role in deciding nominations, but in enhancing their influence in exchanges with candidates, on the one hand, and voters, on the other. The provision of money and services to officeholders will increase the influence of party committees to the extent those candidates are not able to develop those resources independently. By happy accident for those who would strengthen parties, the bulwarks against the flows of political money erected by the recent finance legislation offer the prospect of opening the floodgates for party money while maintaining the dikes limiting other channels available to candidates. Doing so would have a reasonable probability of bringing party interests at least up to parity with interest group politics in their claim on the attention span of officeholders.

Financially robust parties could also have some influence upon voters' perceptions of the stakes in electoral competition. Through direct mail solicitations, get-out-the-vote efforts, and party-oriented advertising, party money could promote a greater sense among voters of the collective responsibility of officeholders as party nominees. Here again, an instrumental use of the finance laws is required, for totally eliminating the restrictions on direct party help to their candidates would remove the incentive for developing innovative ways of spending money on party-enhancing activities.

The conception of party committees as something like super PACs should be taken as a description of the direction in which they are changing today. As a statement of what parties ought to become, however, the model has two serious limitations which should be explicitly recognized. The first of these is an outgrowth of the nationalizing trend; the second results from the technology being pressed into service of parties.

In each state, party coalitions have developed out of a history of political competition grappling with a somewhat unique inventory of problems. The Democratic party of Alabama, for ex-

ample, embraces a very different clientele, built upon a different
political discourse, than does the Democratic party of Massa-
chusetts. Into this diversity step the national parties attempting
to promote national agendas and a national conception of party.
But, the sum total of adherents to a national party in each state
is certainly less than the number of party faithful enlisted by
the contours of local political fissures. There is, thus, a tension
between strong national parties and strong state parties which
cannot be ignored or eliminated. To the extent that national
parties are able to exploit economies of scale in the technologies
of communication and thereby override more local identities, they
will weaken state parties politically. Stronger parties offer no sure
escape from the problems of federalism.

The potential future for parties I have drawn here should set
off a second alarm bell somewhere in our thinking. Parties have
always been instruments for involving citizens directly in politics
and promoting face-to-face contact. Yet the new technologies
promote a remoteness to political dialogue that is potentially
alienating. For the voter, will the combination of listening to
a paid advertisement, responding to a direct mail solicitation,
and answering an opinion poll be as satisfying as an opportunity
for face-to-face exchange of political ideas? I doubt it, and I worry
for the vitality of our politics if that's all that parties provide.

Providing one accepts both the benefits of party committees as
broader PACs and the limitations upon our expectations, there
are improvements in the campaign laws that will direct more
money through parties and, thereby, strengthen them. Basically,
the current laws could be amended to increase the money flowing
through the party committees, while simultaneously restricting
the torrent of PAC money.

A first step would be to allow parties to take in greater amounts.
The arguments for maintaining strict limits on contributions to
candidates and political committees rest primarily on the need
to prevent corruption of the political process or even the appearance of corruption which can erode citizen confidence in the
electoral system. These are important values to be safeguarded,
but they are less cogent, in my view, when considering money
directed through party channels. In the first place, our measure-
ment of what constitutes *undue* influence should be more expansive for parties than for wealthy private citizens or narrow

interest groups. Secondly, since money given through parties is less direct, the corruption argument is less weighty. (Contributions through parties which are "earmarked" for specific candidates should be illegal.)

The limitation on individual contributions to party committees could be increased and exempted from an individual's overall contribution limitation. Similarly, the ceiling on PAC giving to parties could be increased dramatically (from $15,000 to $50,000, for example). And the tax credit for small contributions could be simultaneously increased to 100 percent of the contribution and reserved for giving to party committees (or candidates and party committees).

At the same time, party committees could be gradually allowed to contribute more and spend more on behalf of their candidates. (This suggestion is probably more acceptable if implemented in gradual steps. Given the present disparities between the two parties, proposals for an immediate increase in party money will be viewed with a good deal of suspicion.)

If a great deal more money can be directed through the party channel, the change might release some of the pressure now building to change the act in other ways: pressure due to the difficulties of raising adequate funds, the greater reliance upon PAC money, and the increasing recourse to independent expenditures. In the eight years since enactment, it has become clear that the laws require some major adjustments. These proposals might improve the function of the finance laws, while aiding the development of stronger party committees.

At the same time, these changes would make party money a more valuable prize to control. If party support to candidates became unlimited while other conduits were restricted, incumbent legislators would certainly become interested in capturing the campaign committees. It may be that the primary reason why the Republican committees can exercise wide latitude in targeting resources is related to the ability of the party's incumbents to draw upon ample funds from other sources. An incumbent President might also be tempted to use the national committee to try to get control of the money flowing through the campaign committees. For this reason, the "agency agreements," whereby state parties designate the national campaign committee as their agent to spend their allotment of "coordinated expenditures," should be prohibited. While it is certainly valuable to increase the leverage available to Presidents and congressional leadership, the balance point should not be moved so far that national forces completely override those of states and localities. Therefore, party money should also be channeled through state party institutions.

On the presidential level, the limitations of expenditures ought to be abolished for a host of reasons, but the most convenient way of accomplishing that change would be by allowing parties to raise and spend unlimited amounts in the general election. While the parties probably would never be able to bring much pressure to bear on an incumbent President, the effect of this change would be to allow parties to use their presidential candidates as a means of maintaining a robust fund-raising apparatus. In addition, party committees ought to be allowed to spend money on behalf of presidential candidates during the prenomination period, but this change should be coupled with elimination of the spending limits which now regulate presidential candidates in the primaries.

Finally, since parties are most directly in competition with interest groups for influence over public officeholders, the law could be altered in ways that would benefit parties by diminishing the flow of money through PACs. For example, the ceiling on contributions to candidates by PACs could be lowered, perhaps even cut in half. The tax credit for contributions to political action committees could be eliminated. If paired with an increase in the amounts PACs can contribute to party committees, lower limits might not result in a huge increase in independent spending.

Summary

The national party committees do appear to be gaining some strength through successful exploitation of the opportunities provided by the campaign finance laws. The evidence is not entirely unambiguous, however, since most of the successes have occurred on the Republican side. But even the Democratic party is in better financial shape now than at any time since the 1968 campaign, and the staff which took over after the 1980 election has vowed maximum efforts to catch up.

This recent strength is not a return to anything we have experienced, especially on the national level where parties have never been strong. The basis of party influence, if it exists, is the command over electoral resources valuable to politicians. It might well be possible to change the finance laws in ways that would give parties an even larger proportion of the funds raised by candidates. Such a change would be beneficial, particularly if it allowed candidates to raise ample funds without having to rely upon PACs. However, the available evidence should caution us that the laws cannot quickly alter the distribution of political power among electoral institutions. For example, if vastly greater funds were directed through the party channels, incumbents would probably exercise greater influence over the party decisions on allocating that money.

In the long run, however, it seems preferable to direct more money through party institutions, since, by their nature, they provide pressure toward coalition-building and policy consensus across a range of issues rather than the fragmentation and compartmentalization of different policy problems generated by interest group politics. In short, the best way to make party leadership a significant counterbalance to interest groups is to allow party committees to become a more significant factor in election financing. Given the increasing reliance upon PAC contributions, party money appears to be the best alternative means for providing adequate campaign resources to those candidates who would prefer to avoid the money that comes with interest group strings attached. While it cannot be a cure-all, a higher degree of party participation in the financing of electoral politics will work in the direction of facilitating coherent governance.

Pope McCorkle and Joel L. Fleishman

5

Political Parties
and Presidential Nominations

The Intellectual Ironies of Reform and Change
in the Mass Media Age

Introduction

Critical discourse about the presidential nominating process
usually goes off in one of two directions. One approach concentrates on the "ideal type" of political structure for selection of
the President. It features dispassionate but conflicting discussion
about the kinds of political values that should be maximized in
the process: the clash between the virtues of popular participation
versus institutional party mediation is perhaps the most familiar
theme in the literature. The other approach focuses on the
actual "making of a President" and how the nominating structure

POPE MCCORKLE *is executive assistant of the Forum on Presidential Nominations at the Institute of Policy Sciences and Public Affairs at Duke University.
He was previously associated with the National Broadcasting Corporation as
an election researcher and with the John and Mary R. Markle Foundation
as a research assistant.*

favors the political jockeying of one kind of candidate over another. In this chapter we hope to benefit from the insights of both approaches without suffering from the pitfalls of either.

For the last few decades most discussion about the presidential nominating process has either explicitly or implicitly focused on the Democratic party. Some commentators have sardonically suggested that this monopoly of critical concern explains why the Democratic party finds itself in worse shape than its Republican counterpart. It is both more sobering and accurate to recognize that so much critical attention has been spent on the Democrats because the party of the New Deal has represented the majority coalition and thus the more decisive element in the governing of society. While this chapter does not strain to pretend that the Republican nominating process has figured as significantly in the minds of most participants in the debate, we do believe that such new factors as the influence of the mass media over the nominating process make it easier to generalize about the situation in both parties.

In considering the fate of the nominating process, one must always realize that the nomination of candidates for President and other elected offices is and always has been the raison d'être of American political parties. And because the presidential nominating process plays a vital role in determining *who* eventually gets elected, such discussion always involves the large question of governance. In examining differing viewpoints about the nominating process, we have tried to keep these larger issues in mind.

This chapter does not pretend to be an exercise in political engineering which deals with the nuts and bolts of the nominating structure. We do make a set of general recommendations that borrows from and synthesizes aspects of the most prominent models in contemporary intellectual debate. But our main goal is to place discussion about the presidential nominating process in the larger historical and political context from which it springs. We think that this effort is especially important because views concerning the presidential nominating process and political parties seem to be undergoing unprecedented and quite ironic transformations in the early 1980s.

The Intellectual Conflict over the Primary System and the Institutional Party in the Progressive Era

"One of the objections that is always made to the direct primary is that it takes away party responsibility and breaks down party control. But this objection thus given against the direct primary I frankly offer as one of the best reasons for its retention," declared Senator George Norris in the *Annals of the American Academy of Political Science* in 1923. During the first part of the twentieth century, most political reformers shared the maverick Nebraska senator's positive view of the primary and negative view of the institutional party. These reformist views of primaries and parties were central elements of the "Progressive" ideology for governing the country. As Richard Hofstadter explained in his classic study *The Age of Reform*:

> Democracy was considered to require not merely competition between party organizations that would afford the voters a choice, but rank-and-file control or dissolution of the organizations themselves. The movement for the direct primary was the chief embodiment of this conception of democracy.

The father of the primary movement is widely acknowledged to be reform Governor Robert M. LaFollette, Sr. of Wisconsin. After pushing through legislation in 1905 providing for the direct election of Wisconsin delegates to the national party conventions, LaFollette proclaimed that "no longer . . . will there stand between the voter and the official a political machine with a complicated system of caucuses and conventions, by the manipulation of which it thwarts the will of the voter and rules of official conduct." The Progressive primary movement reached its high tide when Teddy Roosevelt called for a national presidential primary in the 1912 campaign and Woodrow Wilson formally proposed a national primary plan in his first annual message to Congress in 1913.

This political vision was obviously not accepted by either the stalwart conservatives or the machine politicians of the era. In defense of the party system, Tammany Hall sage George Washington Plunkitt thought that he had "some arguments that nobody could answer":

First, this great and glorious country was built up by political parties; second, parties can't hold together if their workers don't get offices when they win; third, if the parties go to pieces, the government they built up must go to pieces, too; fourth, then there'll be hell to pay.

And Boss Tweed of Tammany Hall himself underscored the importance of control over the nominating process in declaring that "I don't care who does the electing, so long as I can do the nominating." Like the leaders of any other "private" organization, the party bosses resisted any reform effort that would allow government or reform groups to interfere with their decision-making power.

Ironically enough, the machine politicians of Tammany Hall were the degenerate heirs of a party system which one of its prime proponents, Martin Van Buren, had proudly called "a radical reform" in the nineteenth century. Furthermore, as Hofstadter, Robert Dahl, and others have pointed out, merely the belief that the political system could survive the conflict between opposing parties represented an unparalleled "liberal" or "progressive" leap forward in the history of Western democracy. But it is certainly not unusual in America for the reform programs of one era to be used for conservative ends in a later one, as well as vice versa.

Toward an Emerging Intellectual Realignment in the 1980s?

After an initially overwhelming wave of popular enthusiasm for primaries and "direct democracy" in general, the conservative party bosses were able to stem the tide between World Wars I and II. Yet by 1980 the old Progressive vision of reform had triumphed to such an extent that primaries were commonplace in contests for major state-wide political offices and had come to dominate the nomination process for presidential candidates. The increase in the number of presidential primaries has been especially dramatic over the last two decades. In 1960 presidential primaries were held in sixteen states. But in 1980 the number of primaries had more than doubled to thirty-six, and the presidential preferences of approximately 75 percent of the delegates to the Democratic and Republican national conventions were determined in primaries. Moreover, in the 1970s a new round of proposals for a national (and regional) presidential primary system was introduced in Congress.

It would be tempting to suppose that contemporary liberal reformers would be preparing for the ultimate triumph of national primary legislation in the 1980s. The startling fact is, however, that a number of contemporary liberal intellectuals and reformers have expressed neither enthusiastic nor even lukewarm support but downright hostility toward any movement in the direction of a national primary. "A national primary, . . ." declared Arthur Schlesinger, Jr. in *The Wall Street Journal* in 1979, "must be resisted." Instead, according to Schlesinger, "We should do what we can to avoid weakening the party system further."

Some liberals go so far as to wish for the abolition of primaries. "Primaries have ruined our politics" was the plaintive lead that *The New Republic* chose for an article on the state of the American political condition after the 1980 election by contributing editor Michael Walzer, a noted liberal-left political theorist at the Institute for Advanced Study. In *The New Republic* article Walzer identified himself as a supporter of recent liberal-insurgent candidacies beginning with that of Eugene McCarthy in 1968. But Walzer's article seemed to represent a belated liberal intellectual confirmation of the practical warning from Tammany's Plunkitt that "there'll be hell to pay" if plebiscitary politics overcome the party system. Declared Walzer:

> The defenders of primaries have never come to grips with the requirements of a party system. . . . The purpose of a party system is to provide us with candidates who represent a certain set of interests, not some random, self-selected portion of the general electorate. . . . Only candidates like this [*party candidates*] can govern effectively. . . .

Five years before Walzer's article, another prominent liberal academic and supporter of reform politics, Professor Wilson Carey McWilliams, sounded the same themes in an article entitled "Down with Primaries" for the liberal periodical *Commonweal*. McWilliams restated his position that "primaries are out of the question" in an essay for a collection entitled *Party Renewal in America* published in 1980. Similarly, the late *Nation* editor Carey McWilliams echoed his son's sentiments in 1979 by asserting that restoration of a nominating system with "a measure of give-and-take and consultation and negotiation" among party leaders and delegates at the national convention "would be preferable to the primary system as it functions today."

Similar sentiments were also expressed by prominent figures within the presidential nomination reform movement of the Democratic party. "I have to admit," stated former South Dakota Senator George McGovern in *Time*, "that the more primaries there are, the more difficult is the process." In the same vein former Democratic Minnesota Congressman Donald Fraser declared at a 1979 symposium on political parties that presidential primaries are "awful things" and that "a large number of party activists who have classified themselves as reformers . . . are concerned about this proliferation of presidential primaries."

One would expect that cries for retrenchment by liberal reformers would play into the hands of conservative stalwarts. While there are few figures still remaining who are willing to defend an unreconstructed Tammany Hall view of politics, there are a number of influential conservative commentators who have always taken great delight in criticizing the consequences of reformers' disruption of the political status quo. It stands to reason that these conservative critics would be reveling in the acknowledgment by liberal reformers that institutional party control is superior to the kind of plebiscitary politics exemplified by the primary.

Yet as the presidential election of 1980 approached, serious discussion about congressional legislation to establish a modified form of the national presidential primary system developed in influential conservative circles. In the spring of 1980 *Fortune* published an article on the presidential nominating process by "neoconservative" political scientist Everett Carll Ladd entitled "A Better Way to Pick Our President." In laying out his proposal Ladd stated:

> We must begin by recognizing that the presidential primaries are here to stay. It is naive indeed to expect their use to be rolled back. . . . Congress should enact legislation requiring both parties to choose delegates to the national conventions through nationally structured primaries to be held on a single day. . . .

While 66 percent of the convention delegates would be bound on the first ballot in proportion to the percentage of major candidates' votes in the simultaneously held state primaries, Ladd did reserve a somewhat counterbalancing role for major state party and elected officials, who would comprise the final third of the delegates and be formally uncommitted to any candidate. Ladd acknowledged, however, that the national primary day could virtually determine the party nominee: "A candidate who ran very strongly in the national primary would almost surely add enough support from party leaders to be nominated on the first ballot [at the convention]."

In "A Better Way to Pick Our President" Ladd took special note of the assistance given in the refinement of his modified national primary proposal by two scholars-in-residence at the American Enterprise Institute (AEI), Austin Ranney and Thomas Mann. And the modified national primary plan was a major topic at the subsequent roundtable discussion among the members of the neoconservative think tank's Program in Political and Social Processes, which was published in pamphlet form as *The Presidential Nominating Process: Can It Be Improved?* Opinions ranged from Professor Mann's outright support to Professor (now U.N. Ambassador) Jeane Kirkpatrick's dissent. Yet the general consensus that moderator Ranney spotted among the group was almost as noteworthy as unanimous support for the national primary plan would have been. For Ranney pointed out that "we all agree that whatever system is adopted ought to be a *national system . . . mandated by Congress* [emphasis added]." Kirkpatrick's alternative plan, for instance, proposed congressional legislation to *ban* all primaries and require that all national convention delegates be party leaders or elected officials. As Ranney had argued in his previous work, any such nationalization by congressional legislation or "federalization" of the presidential primary process would entail a historic shift in institutional control of the party system's nominating process to the popularly elected legislative branch of the federal government. Thus the Kirkpatrick proposal represents nearly as significant a departure from the traditional belief of party stalwarts in "private" or nongovernmental control of the party system as does Ladd's proposal for national primary legislation.

At the AEI symposium Professor Ranney refrained from endorsing either the Ladd or Kirkpatrick proposal but predicted that "every four years a few more states will add primaries until in 1984 or 1988 forty-seven or forty-eight states will have primaries. At some point—probably before this century is out—

Congress will adopt some form of a national primary." During another discussion in late 1979 Ranney was quoted in the *New York Times* as stating that a congressionally mandated national primary scheme "would certainly be better than what we have now."

It would be too fast and easy to conclude that a great intellectual inversion has taken place wherein the liberals have become the elitists and the conservatives are the populists. Furthermore, there are certainly those on the left who cling to the old Progressive faith in primaries, and those on the right who still adhere to traditional beliefs about the need for unquestioned control by the institutional party leadership. Similarly, the revisions in intellectual viewpoints should not be confused with majority opinion in either the Republican or Democratic party. Yet it may also be wrong to dismiss this change as mere tactical posturing due to the liberal disillusionment with the triumph of Jimmy Carter in 1976 or the conservative euphoria over the coming of the "Reagan Revolution" in 1980. Instead the emergence of these new positions on presidential primaries and institutional party control may well be part of a larger intellectual realignment of liberal and conservative visions about how the country should be governed. Liberal reformers and intellectuals are starting to voice an appreciation for a number of those "mediating" political institutions which their predecessors scorned as elitist tools for the governing of society. At the same time a number of contemporary conservatives are apparently beginning to modify their traditional belief in the need for the preeminence of such institutions in favor of accepting more direct links between "the people" and their elected representatives.

This process of realignment is also evident, for example, in recent discussions concerning the courts and the practice of judicial review. Progressive reformers used to excoriate the courts as well as the parties for the frustration of the popular will. Institutional party control over the presidential nomination process and the judicial veto of "social" legislation were both considered to be exercises of power with no constitutional justification at all. Conservatives meanwhile defended both institutions as indispensable instruments in controlling the irrationalities of majoritarian democracy. Yet in recent years, as with the case of the institutional party, many liberals have backed off from the old

antagonism toward the courts. These reformers now whole-
heartedly approve of judicial review (and judicial action in general) as a tool to protect and improve the social position of
various minorities. Conversely, neoconservatives (as well as those
farther on the right) rail at the "imperial judiciary" and its lack
of political accountability to mass public opinion.

The Dissolution of the Semisovereign Synthesis

Regardless of whether this realignment in intellectual opinion evolves further in the 1980s, the recent espousal of rather
untraditional notions does prove that intellectual thought about
the presidential nominating process and the parties is in a state
of flux. It provides, if nothing else, some convincing evidence of
the dissolution of the post–World War II intellectual synthesis
that promised to negotiate a workable compromise between the
old Progressive faith in "the people" and the conservative belief
in the mediating role of the parties and other political institutions. The nature of this intellectual synthesis and the history of
its demise are essential in understanding new intellectual views
concerning the nominating process.

The terms of the post–World War II synthesis were the work
of a number of prestigious organizations and eminent individuals.
For the purposes of this discussion, however, a handful of intellectual figures can be chosen as most representative—political
scientist Robert Dahl, historian Richard Hofstadter, and legal
scholar Alexander Bickel. They belonged somewhere on the left
side of the political spectrum, but all three made a self-conscious
effort to reconcile the plebiscitary instincts of Progressivism with
conservative wisdom about the moderating virtues of institutions
in politics. As Hofstadter believed about reformers, "Many of us
have in the past made a mystique of the masses and have tended
too much to attribute all the villainy in our world to the machina-
tions of vested interests."

There were many subtle and not-so-subtle differences among
these thinkers. Yet with all proper deference to such differences,
it can still be said that all of them helped shape a political formulation which envisioned the relationship of the people to political
institutions as one of "semisovereignty." The ultimate legitimacy
of the political system would rest on a mass base that would never-

theless be mediated by the leadership of the two major parties and in extreme circumstances be subject to the veto review of such elite institutions as the courts. This kind of political system, according to Dahl in *Who Governs?*, would allow most citizens "a moderate degree of indirect influence" over the direction of government policy between elections.

The authors have borrowed the word "semisovereign" from E. E. Schattschneider's *The Semi-Sovereign People* (1960). Schattschneider's formulation, however, differed somewhat from that of the other mentioned thinkers by decrying the "semisovereignty" of the people and pointing to strong political parties as the instrument to cure this political condition. Although Schattschneider's view enjoyed a good deal of support in the political science profession, we believe that the views of these other thinkers were more influential in the larger intellectual environment. We have chosen to use the "semisovereign synthesis" to describe the other political thinkers' formulation, because the phrase is more evocative than the usual description of their thinking as "pluralism" or "elitist theory of democracy."

Recent years have subjected this conservative-Progressive synthesis to both penetrating as well as widely off-the-mark criticism. The very persistence of criticism from left and right is itself persuasive proof that the "semisovereign" architects underestimated the continued vitality of dissenting ideologies in American political life. The lessons that such thinkers believed American politics should have drawn from the horrible ideological excesses and resulting atrocities of Nazi Germany and Stalinist Russia were not so much unlearned as simply considered irrelevant to the American experience. But more important to the demise of the semisovereign synthesis than the failure to recognize the continuance of ideology was an aspect of American political life that all these thinkers knew could doom their vision: the egalitarian instinct in the American populace that Alexis de Tocqueville had observed as long ago as the 1830s in his observation on *Democracy in America*. The proponents of the semisovereign synthesis hoped that the establishment of the New Deal's welfare state would satisfy or at least keep in check this deep-seated impulse, but the promise of the affluent society after World War II actually fueled a new wave of egalitarian desire. The combination of political ideology with the renewed egalitarian impulse reached an explosive fruition in what is now symbolically referred to as "the sixties"—which stands for the historical moment when almost all established institutions seemed in danger of being permanently overrun. Although the egalitarian and ideological outbursts are sometimes exclusively associated with movements of the political left, the fact is that these powerful forces were also evident—even if dressed up in a rather different garb—among the following of George Wallace and the members of the "silent majority" on the right. It is not surprising that Hofstadter bitterly (and unfairly) referred to the decade as "the age of rubbish."

The dashing of the semisovereign synthesis was manifested most clearly within the Democratic party. Most of these post–World War II intellectual figures viewed the Democratic party as playing the most crucial role in representing and mediating the demands of the mass base of the post–New Deal political system. And in 1960 the contest for the party's presidential nomination resembled an almost perfect approximation of the semisovereign vision. The primary battles between Senator Kennedy and Senator Humphrey were between two relatively experienced Washington officeholders while a number of other experienced politicians—former Democratic nominee Adlai Stevenson, Lyndon B. Johnson, and Stuart Symington—were waiting in the wings. In each of the handful of important contests, the primary candidates were faced with what Teddy White in *The Making of the President, 1960* called a "sense of multiple audience"—the need to win over not simply the primary electorate but also the state party leaders across the nation. In contrast to the almost total concentration on the winning of convention delegates in the more than thirty primaries in 1980, the garnering of convention delegates in the handful of 1960 primaries was of secondary importance. As David Broder has pointed out:

> Kennedy ran in four contested primaries. Contrast that with the thirty-five who await anyone who wants the nomination in 1980. After Kennedy won in West Virginia, he still had to persuade the leaders of his party . . . that they could stake their reputation on his qualities as the best man to be the standard bearer of the party. Contrast that with Jimmy Carter, who never had to meet, and in fact did not meet, those similar officials until after he had achieved the Democratic nomination.

Moreover, in discussing the 1960 nomination campaign, Kennedy could sound like a perfect model of acceptance concerning the semisovereignty of "the people" in the nomination process. White recounts, for instance, that after analyzing his chances for a victory in the Wisconsin primary, Kennedy immediately

> made a transit to the big bosses who would control the convention—he mused on the effect a victory here would have on the thinking of Governor Lawrence, boss of vital Pennsylvania, from that he made the transit to the similarity of Lawrence's problems in Pennsylvania to the problems of Governor Rossellini in the State of Washington. . . .

Yet the Kennedy campaign of 1960 also presaged the eventual dissolution of the semisovereign vision. For at certain times it seemed that Kennedy wanted not merely to impress but to overwhelm the established party leadership. White noted that Kennedy enjoyed the image of the young prince running against the party barons, and Arthur Schlesinger has quoted him as bragging to Stevenson on the eve of the 1960 convention that "the support of leaders is much overrated anyway; leaders aren't worth a damn." Moreover, according to White, "nothing seemed preposterous" about primary campaigning to Kennedy, who "felt that running for the Presidency was his most important full-time business and Senate attendance took second place." In contrast, his main primary opponent, Humphrey, longed to be back in Washington. As Humphrey lamented before switching to another issue at a press conference before the Wisconsin primary, "Any man who goes into a primary isn't *fit* to be President. You have to be crazy to go into a primary. A primary, now, is worse than the torture of the rack. It's all right to enter a primary by accident, or because you don't know any better, but by forethought. . . ." For the next two decades it was the harrassed Humphrey—the loyal party man struggling vainly to capture the popular imagination—who would epitomize the failed vision of the semisovereign synthesis.

The restless antiinstitutionalism glimpsed in John F. Kennedy's 1960 campaign seemed to overflow with the emergence of his brother Robert Kennedy's vision of the "New Politics" in the 1968 campaign. "Our strategy," proclaimed young R.F.K. aide Adam Walinsky, "is to change the rules of nominating a President. We're going to do it a new way. In the streets." Yet the younger Kennedy's "New Politics" did not simply envision the enshrinement of a Rousseauean general will; it also contained the hope of somehow mastering the contradictory whirls of discontent

surrounding the issues of civil rights, law and order, the Vietnam
War, and the larger crisis of confidence tearing apart the political
institutions of American society. As Professor Nelson Polsby has
written, in an as yet unpublished manuscript on party reform,
"[Robert] Kennedy represented not an antiestablishment but an
alternative establishment." Thus even such a moderate believer
in the semisovereignty of the people as Alexander Bickel proudly
acknowledged that he "followed Robert Kennedy in 1968, heart
and mind." Bickel explained in *The New Republic* that Robert
Kennedy appeared to be the politician most capable of holding
the post–World War II political vision together: "I believed he
[R.F.K.] had come to know better and more deeply than anyone
how dangerously we are nearing a dead end. . . . He had the trust
of those whom we desperately need. . . ." And the McGovern-
Fraser reform commission, which has been accused of trying to
transform the Democratic party structure and nominating process
according to the most radical version of the "New Politics" creed,
actually betrayed some of Bickel's hopes that reform could salvage
what remained of the mediating force in the two-party system:

> If we are not an open party, if we do not represent the demands of
> change, then the danger is not that people will go to the Republican
> Party; it is that there will no longer be a way for people committed to
> orderly change to fulfill their needs and desires within our traditional
> political system. It is that they will turn to third and fourth party politics
> or the antipolitics of the street.

The grand vision of the "New Politics" hardly reinvigorated
the semisovereign synthesis or ushered in a new era of political
harmony. In its efforts to open up the avenues of "orderly change"
within the Democratic party, the McGovern-Fraser commission
reforms alienated a number of the relatively conservative and
moderate members of the synthesis. An especially important symbolic event was the unceremonious ejection of Mayor Daley and
his Cook County delegation at the 1972 national convention. The
subsequent nomination of the former chairman of the reform
commission, George McGovern, proved controversial enough to
help drive the last nail in the coffin of the semisovereign synthesis. While venerable figures like Dahl, Arthur Schlesinger, Jr.,
and John Kenneth Galbraith basically approved of the reform
movement as an essential attempt to renew the Democratic party's
connection with its mass base, most of those figures closer to
Hofstadter and Bickel (who suffered untimely deaths) came to the

conclusion that the Democratic party had recklessly devalued the mediating role of the established party leadership. The synthesis had basically split into two warring intellectual factions—New Liberals and New Conservatives.

The Reversal of Intellectual Positions: Reformers as Party Insiders and Conservatives as Party Outsiders

It is inevitable that the New Liberals would portray their intellectual opponents as apologists of the old Tammany Hall view of politics and the New Conservative intellectuals would return the compliment by painting the reform movement as the reincarnation of the old Progressivism. Both sides took some pleasure in playing out such roles for the sake of polemical combat. In reality, however, the political situation had been turned upside down from the Progressive era. Despite the continuance of its outsider rhetoric, the reform movement defended by the New Liberals had ascended to a position of virtual leadership status in the Democratic party. Although the left wing insurgency's outright control of the party proved temporary, it still had enough muscle to remain a significant force throughout the 1970s. On the other hand, the New Conservatives had moved to a position of antagonism toward at least one element of the Democratic leadership—and ambivalent leaning toward the Republican party—that ironically resembled the "Mugwumpish" or independent stance of Progressive intellectuals. Because reformers had become the party "insiders," the New Liberal intellectuals could hardly continue to express unqualified beliefs in the classic antiparty vehicle of the primary. By the same token, New Conservative intellectuals found it more difficult to express faith in the mediating virtues of political leadership.

This is not to say that the reform movement's proximity to institutional party control turned New Liberal intellectuals into antidemocratic turncoats. It does mean that the New Liberals naturally tried to square their belief in an "open" and "participatory" nominating process with the fact of reformers' new influence in the Democratic party structure. As one member of the McGovern-Fraser reform commission explained:

> The first thing we members of the Democratic Party's McGovern-Fraser commission (1969–72) agreed on . . . was that we did not want a national presidential primary or any increase in the number of state primaries.

Indeed, we hoped to prevent any such development by reforming the delegate-selection rules so that the party's non-primary processes would be open and fair, participation in them would greatly increase, and consequently the demand for more primaries would fade.

(This account actually comes from New Conservative intellectual Austin Ranney, who became a rather disillusioned member of the commission. Yet the authors do not know of any account which contradicts Ranney's memory on this point.) The alternative nominating structure favored by the liberal reform movement was an updated version of the local party caucus system. These local party meetings would be the bedrock of a nominating system that would eventually send delegates to state and national nominating conventions. Yet, in order to insure that these local party meetings would be conducted in an open and equitable fashion, the reform movement also sought to increase the power of the national committee to police the nominating process. Thus the paradoxical goal was to enhance the political participation of the mass base while at the same time increasing the veto power of the national party leadership.

While the formal power of the national party committee over the nominating process actually expanded in the 1970s, the New Liberal caucus alternative was on the whole not able to satisfy the greater demand of the "people" for participation in the process. The power of the reform movement within the Democratic party weakened as the number of primaries continued to proliferate in the 1970s. Thus New Liberal antipathy to the primary has become even more pronounced. In *Party Renewal in America*, for example, James MacGregor Burns declared:

> The caucus system must be the party's answer—indeed, it is the only feasible answer—to that great institutional enemy of parties, the primary system for choosing party nominees. . . . If primaries appear to bring a measure of intraparty democracy to nomination politics, the caucuses could supply a far superior kind of democracy, measured by intensive voter participation, thorough canvassing of candidates and issues and careful consideration of the present and potential link between a would-be nominee and the party.

It should also not be thought that the New Conservatives' "outsider" party status turned them into uncritical believers in plebiscitary politics. A number of New Conservatives initially reacted by angrily demanding a return to "the good old days" before the 1960s. Professor Kirkpatrick's proposal for congressional legislation to ban all primaries and require only ex officio delegates at the national convention provides a good example of this "turn-back-the-clock" sentiment. Yet some New Conservatives have begun to confront the less dramatic alternatives and find the primary system more tolerable than the new Liberals' party caucus system. According to national primary proponent Everett Carll Ladd:

> The fuzzy romanticism that has been so influential in recent thinking about presidential selection tells us that institutional party life of a sustained sort is possible through *ad hoc* assemblies. That is, the faithful may come together in party caucuses, debate the issues and the merits of the contending candidates, and thus express an *institutional party choice*. This is errant nonsense. Party caucuses in the modern sense are *nothing more than restrictive primaries*. [emphasis in original]

New Conservatives have especially pointed out that the New Liberals' emphasis on participation from such constituencies as blacks, women, and youth at local caucuses tends to exclude and alienate the Democrats' traditional white, blue-collar base—what New Conservative Michael Novak has called "the unmeltable ethnics." Thus New Conservatives have actually found themselves in the position of arguing that the New Liberal caucus system is too elitist. Moreover, the growing conservative tendency of plebiscitary politics in the late 1970s exemplified by California's Proposition 13 has mollified somewhat the New Conservative attitude toward direct democracy. It is doubtful whether the New Conservatives will totally drop their belief in the mediating virtues of established party leadership. In Ladd's modified national primary plan, for example, the minority of uncommitted ex officio delegates would play a key role in brokering the convention if no clear front runner emerged from the national primary. Yet it is still an unmistakable indication of the New Conservatives' "outsider" status that Ladd's proposal—as well as that of Kirkpatrick—envisions the necessity of going *outside* the party structure and asking for congressional legislation.

The New Liberals, the New Conservatives, and the Mass Media

There do not seem to be many significant points of agreement between the New Liberal and New Conservative visions for the presidential nominating process. The New Liberals advocate a party caucus system and reject the plebiscitary trend toward greater use of primaries. The New Conservatives desire control of the party nominating process by Congress, and at least some of these intellectuals believe that the parties should accommodate the plebiscitary trend. Yet at a more general level both sides do agree that the institutional party should play some kind of mediating role in the nominating process. Furthermore, both New Conservatives and New Liberals fear that a new kind of "mediating" institution—the electronic media—is totally displacing the role of the party in the presidential nominating process. As Arthur Schlesinger, Jr. declared at a symposium in 1979:

> The source of our contemporary forebodings lies, I believe, in the electronic revolution of the late twentieth century and in the radical changes wrought by electronic technology in the political environment. . . . Television presents the politician directly to the voter, and the contemporary voters are more likely to make their judgments on what Walter Cronkite and John Chancellor show them than on what the local party . . . leader tells them. Computerized public opinion polls present the voter directly to the politician, and the contemporary politician is more likely to judge opinion by what is read in the polls than what he is told by the local party or other leader. The prime party function . . . described as "brokerage" is becoming obsolete.

And New Conservative Austin Ranney echoed strong agreement:

> Arthur . . . calls our attention to a development that may overshadow everything else we have discussed here. That is the fact that the mass media, and particularly television, have come to be the main channels through which political events are seen and, thus, by which the political reality on which we all act is created. Moreover, as Arthur points out, there is something profoundly antiparty about the manner in which TV presents reality. That is not because of a conspiracy by the broadcasters but because the very nature of TV forces it to focus on the personality, the individual, the unique, the pictorial. . . .

Common recognition of the political importance of television and the rest of the electronic media represents a clear indication of the great social and intellectual changes since the semisovereign thinkers put together their vision of American politics after World War II. For one of the key premises of the semisovereign vision was that "the people" did not accept most political communication generated by the mass media until it was processed or filtered by "influentials" or opinion leaders in the community —who were usually connected with one of the parties or another established political institution. Thus the system of political communication represented a "two-step" process which was first mediated by political elites before being passed on to the masses. This "two-step" theory was popularized by communications scholar Paul Lazarsfeld—another key figure in the semisovereign synthesis—and his associates in such works as *Personal Influence: The Part Played by People in the Flow of Mass Communications* (1955).

Like the whole semisovereign synthesis itself, it is difficult to separate the *actual description of* from the *ideal prescription for* post–World War II society in this "two-step" theory of political communication. Yet the massive empirical study of *The American Voter* published in 1960 by the distinguished team of social researchers at the University of Michigan's Survey Research Center seemed to provide strong validation for the general "two-step" belief that political parties represented strong screening forces in the formulation of political attitudes among the mass base of the political system. Regardless of the theory's accuracy at its inception, however, the emerging consensus among political scholars as well as practitioners from various perspectives is that the political parties do not now serve as significant mediators of political information and that the mass media are increasingly taking over the function of organizing and managing the political arena. The empirical study of *The Changing American Voter* published by a distinguished team of Harvard political scientists in 1979 found not a system dominated by the political parties but a "system of individualistic voting choice between ad hoc electoral organizations . . . mediated by television." In his unpublished manuscript, Professor Nelson Polsby has similarly stated that "for good or ill a political system having intermediation process heavily reliant upon the mass media is the sort of political system that is emerging in the U.S." During the 1980 campaign experienced practitioners in campaign politics stated the proposition even more bluntly: "The news media," wrote campaign manager John Sears in *The Washington Journalism Review*, "control the nomination and election of the President today." Knowledgeable newspeople did not deny the charge as much as try to turn it back around on the candidates and their managers: "The power of the news media, . . ." replied Daniel Schorr in another magazine, "is wielded for the most part not by journalistic practitioners. . . . It is wielded, rather, by politicians and their media advisers, who have learned to exploit a potent medium."

The rise of television as the preeminent medium for campaign and political news has confirmed the demise of the "two-step" theory of political communication. It is not accidental that the beginning of television's dominance can be traced back to the 1960s when the restless antiinstitutional impulses of the post–World War II era exploded with such unexpected force against established institutions. As journalist Nicholas Lemann has written, "At the same time that traditional conduits from politicians to voters were cracking, a new conduit was emerging: television. In 1950, 9 percent of American households had televisions; in 1960, 87 percent; in 1970, 95 percent." In *Press, Party, and the Presidency* Richard Rubin has explained that the *nationalizing* impact of network television overwhelmed the assumed equilibrium of institutional power between the print press and political parties:

> Before television expanded the impact of the press as a whole, a rough balance existed between the print mass media and the political system. Both were strongly localistic, and there was little if any direct, unmediated contact between national leaders and local audiences. But the rise of the electronic media has exacerbated tensions in the relationships between new centralized mass media institutions and still decentralized, fragmented, political and governmental institutions, established in an entirely different environment of informational and political expectation.

Perfect symbols of television's institutional clash with the party system occurred at the 1964 Republican and 1968 Democratic national conventions. The confrontation with the Republican party occurred during a speech by former President Dwight D. Eisenhower. In *The Pulse of Politics: Electing Presidents in a Media Age* Professor James David Barber has told the story particularly well:

> In the midst of his speech [*Eisenhower declared*], "Let us particularly scorn the divisive efforts of those outside our family, including sensation-seeking columnists and commentators,"—and suddenly the galleries and the delegates on the floor erupted in an enormous and unstoppable roar

of angry agreement. When the noise at last subsided, Ike finished his sentence: "—because, my friends, I assure you that these are people who couldn't care less about the good of our party," at which the roars rolled forth again. . . . When at last the furor died down, the reading of the platform went forward. . . . Brinkley switched to his colleague John Chancellor on the floor of the convention. Chancellor loomed up on the screen, saying, "Well, I'd try if I could, David, but I wonder if I may be under arrest." The television audience saw Chancellor, in respectable suit and tie, being forceably carried out of the hall, reporting as he went, "This is John Chancellor, somewhere in custody."

At the bloody 1968 Democratic National Convention, the conflict was capsulized in an incident involving Walter Cronkite and Dan Rather. According to Barber:

One night at the Democratic convention his [*Walter Cronkite's*] CBS colleague Dan Rather was slugged by one of Mayor Daley's goons. Cronkite's voice shook as he said—on camera—"It looks like we've got a bunch of thugs in here," and, "If this sort of thing continues, it makes us in our anger, want to pack up our microphones and typewriters and get the devil out of this town and leave the Democrats to their agony."

It was probably beyond the power of any mediating institution to channel the convulsive conflicts of the 1960s. Yet, according to many observers, television has made a critical contribution in reroutinizing the political process in its aftermath. Wrote sociologist Todd Gitlin in *The Whole World Is Watching: Mass Media in the Making and Unmaking of the New Left*:

Consumer activists, environmentalists, gay activists, feminists, pro and antibusing people, as well as antiabortionists, Jarvis-Gann supporters, Laetrile legalizers, angry loggers, farmers and truck drivers—many movements which can be presented as working for (or against) concrete assimilable reforms have become regular, recognizable, even stock characters in . . . news broadcasts. The media spread the news that alternative opinions exist on virtually every issue. They create an impression that the society is full of political vitality, that interests and opinion contend freely.

Alternative Models for the Nominating Process

THE MASS MEDIA "INDIVIDUALISTIC-MARKETPLACE" MODEL

Critics from diverse perspectives emphasize that there is a good deal of illusion in what Gitlin carefully called the "impression" that the mass media neutrally present an open political arena where various candidate and issue groups can compete on an equal footing. Nevertheless this criticism does not cancel the appropriateness of borrowing loosely from economic terminology to suggest that mass media nominating politics can best be labeled as a "marketplace" model. For only the most dogged laissez-faire believers would insist that any marketplace has to represent a state of perfect competition. The relative marketplace character of mass media politics is especially evident when contrasted with the virtually "oligopolistic" influence of the two major political parties in the old semisovereign ideal.

An economic model of American electoral politics was propounded as long ago as the 1950s by Anthony Downs in *An Economic Theory of Democracy* and has been elaborately refined by adherents to the so-called "rational choice" political school. This model goes so far as to characterize the party as an organization with the characteristics of a consumer-product firm. Recent research on the "professionalization" of the party organization at the national level as well as state level gives some support to the notion of the party's emerging function as an entrepreneurial firm. Yet the logic of a pure mass media marketplace model eventually leads to a more "individualistic" model—what Walter Dean Burnham has called "politics without parties." Scholars as well as practitioners agree that this process seems to be unfolding as individual candidate organizations and independent single-issue groups displace the official party organizations and actually serve as the main entrepreneurial firms in the electoral marketplace. In *The New Republic* Michael Walzer rather caustically described the process:

> The candidate . . . solicits votes among all the registered voters, without regard to their attachment to the party, interest in or loyalty to its programs, or willingness to work for its success. In turn, the voters encounter the candidate only in their living rooms, on the television screen. . . . Voting itself is lifted out of the context of parties and platforms. It is more like impulse buying than political decisionmaking. The expert in advertising is the most important advisor a candidate can have.

This typical description of marketplace politics rejects the notion that the process necessarily elicits a "rational choice" from voting consumers. Regardless of even the best efforts by journalists to be communicators of "objective" information, the mass media still represent the means of transmission for the marketing strategies and advertising imagery of the candidate organizations. As Rubin has explained:

Competing candidate organizations not only make use of new and old communications processes to reach their electoral "markets," but are also, in fact, part of the communications process itself. Where in the news process candidate organizations leave off and the press begins is not always clear, for the press uses candidates to generate news for its own journalistic purposes while the candidates of necessity must use the press to reach and persuade their potential publics.

It seems unquestionable that the presidential nominating structure in the marketplace model of mass media politics would have to be dominated by the primary process. Other more party-oriented mechanisms would contradict the consumer's apparent sovereignty in making his or her product choice. Thus it is not surprising that a number of scholars have pointed out a direct correlation between the rise of television and the proliferation of primaries. Professor Michael Robinson has provocatively labeled the process as the "Network–New Hampshire" syndrome. "As television news reached preeminence as a news medium in the 1960s, and as television began to shift its focus more toward presidential primaries, . . ." according to Robinson, "state legislators, as a consequence, began adopting presidential primaries." In *Press, Party, and the Presidency* Rubin carefully came to a similar conclusion. After acknowledging that "a thorough examination of network news transcripts from 1967 to 1976 clearly shows that renewed interest and demand for primaries came first from candidates challenging entrenched politicians," Rubin went on to state:

> Rather than initiating renewed interest in primaries, the prime political role of television . . . was in legitimating the primary process as *the* genuinely democratic way to choose convention delegates. The basic political posture of television journalism toward alternative nomination procedures was to favor primaries versus state caucus/convention methods, both in amount of coverage and in the positive nature of story treatment. . . . [emphasis in original]

THE NEW CONSERVATIVE "PARTY-PROTECTIONIST" MODEL

When considered against the background of this emerging tendency toward a form of "individualistic-marketplace" politics in the presidential nominating process, the conservative nature of the modified national primary proposal discussed in New Conservative circles becomes plain. Most of these intellectuals have come to the conclusion that the general marketplace trend is inevitable: "My crystal ball tells me," stated Austin Ranney in the *New York Times,* "that over the next 10 . . . [to] 20 years, campaigns will become even more media-dominated, less 'partified,' more candidate-entrepreneurial. . . ." And because of their "independent" status, as well as the apparent conservative mood of the political marketplace, most New Conservatives view the trend with at least more equanimity than in the past. Despite their growing belief that it is no longer feasible to turn back the tide, however, they want to slow down the trend and preserve some measure of a mediating role for the two major parties. Thus Professor Mann commented at the AEI symposium that he supported the modified national primary plan because he feared that "Congress will do away with national conventions and simply have a national primary." Under a full-fledged national primary, party labels would eventually become about as politically significant as the designations American and National League in baseball. There would simply be two separate elections to determine the league winners, followed by a "World Series" between the winning candidates. Yet under the modified New Conservative plan, the nominating conventions would be preserved and the minority of party ex officio delegates could still possibly have an influence on the selection of a nominee. Furthermore, the Ladd proposal would require that all candidates wishing to enter the Democratic or Republican national primary meet the certified standards of that party's national committee or acquire a significant number of signatures from enrolled party members in at least twelve states.

Thus the goal of the New Conservative national primary proposal is to channel the flow of the plebiscitary tide in a fashion that will prolong the political existence of the two major parties. It can be considered a form of "political protectionism" for the two-party system. In order to check the disintegrating tendencies of marketplace politics, the New Conservative idea is to enact congressional legislation which will ensure a formal institutional status for the two major parties in the presidential nominating process. The two parties would become more analogous to public utilities than to autonomous "private" political associations. This kind of "protectionist" solution has been a traditional European response and an increasingly discussed American solution to the problem of declining economic and other social institutions. The "protectionist" nature of the New Conservative vision is further evidenced by Ladd's supplemental proposal in *Fortune* for congressional legislation providing "substantial public funding" of the Democratic and Republican National Committees. Although Ladd does not explicitly say so, the funding of the national committees would apparently serve as a counterforce to present congressional campaign finance legislation which funds candidate organizations directly and thus, according to most observers, encourages the "individualistic-marketplace" trend. The Kirkpatrick alternative also fits this party-protectionist model. Although desiring the repeal rather than the channeling of the plebiscitary trend, it nevertheless calls for congressional legislation which would "nationalize" the major two parties' role in the nominating process.

THE NEW LIBERAL "PARTY COUNTERCULTURAL" MODEL

The New Liberal caucus alternative presents a very different model. It is not totally opposed to some degree of governmental support for the party system. Yet the New Liberal vision calls not for the governmental "nationalization" of the party system but emphasizes that the parties must look, as Wilson Carey McWilliams puts it, to "the private order for its vitality." Moreover, New Liberals display an uncompromising antagonism to the plebiscitary style of mass media marketplace politics. "The 'democratization' of the parties," according to McWilliams,

> . . . does not require primary elections. In fact, if parties wish to retain or regain the allegiance of voters, primary elections are out of the question. Primaries suggest an electorate dominated by the mass media. . . . The new "professionals," the media specialists who shape campaigns, have no ties to particular publics (or even, for that matter, to particular parties); they are part of the mass with which they deal, faceless and unaccountable.

In essence, then, the New Liberal vision can be labeled a "party countercultural" model. Its ideal for the presidential nominating process and the party system is a network of local political cultures and institutions that would be *counter to* or not dependent on the mainstream mass media political culture. As James MacGregor Burns has explained,

> An open caucus must not be merely a ritualistic meeting that partisans attend, but must be a regular set of meetings to which party members

are invited, urged, and politely pressured to attend—meetings in which women, elderly persons, blacks, young people, recent immigrants, and poor persons are made especially welcome—meetings in which major controversial issues are debated. . . .

The party countercultural model obviously borrows some of its inspiration from the left wing political thinking of the 1960s. Yet the New Liberal model also explicitly draws on older political visions. McWilliams, for example, has pointed to the Jeffersonian idea of a "ward system," where (according to Jefferson) "every man is a sharer in the direction of his ward-republic, or some of the higher ones, and feels that he is a participator in the government of affairs, not merely at election one day in the year but every day." In *Party Renewal in America* Burns agreed that such traditional notions about town hall democracy are at the base of the New Liberal model:

> The caucus would help restore a sense of place, of home, of neighborhood, within the parties; could help restore a world of small publics and local politics; could help realize, perhaps, Jefferson's splendid vision of a ward system that, in McWilliams' words, could combine the warm if parochial patriotism of local communities with the broader, more enlightened perspectives of central regimes.

Conclusion: The Vices and Virtues of the New Models

Each of the above mentioned models presents stark alternatives for the future of the parties and the presidential nominating process. Their shortcomings might appear so drastic to those concerned with the governance of society that one may desire some kind of return to the compromise vision of the semisovereign synthesis. Yet it would fall prey to the politics of nostalgia to hope for the restoration of the same vision that once engendered such promise for the reconciliation of "the people" with political institutions. Instead, if a new synthesis is worth attempting, it must try to emulate the post–World War II thinkers by following their strategy of blending elements of the extreme alternatives present in contemporary intellectual opinion. For whatever the deficiencies in the three opposing models, each contains aspects that must be incorporated into any new synthetic vision.

The mass media individualistic-marketplace model, for example, has been roundly criticized as engendering a political structure that is patently incapable of governing society. The traditional worry was that mass media politics would foster larger-than-life demagogues who run roughshod over the office of the President. Yet it now appears that the marketplace politics of the nominating process reduces potential Presidents into smaller-than-life characters in the political equivalent of an often unfunny situation comedy or, even worse, mere consumer products. The eventual choice of the marketplace becomes a slave of his political "Nielsen" ratings and is in constant danger of being *consumed* by public opinion. As Richard Rubin has neatly summarized the charge,

> The weakening of linkages between the political party and the presidency is one of a number of media-related developments that has affected the stability of public confidence in the president's leadership. The weakening of such key political institutions as the parties and the strengthening of the press have, together, contributed to the unmooring of presidential popularity from its traditional anchorages. A new volatility of presidential popularity . . . with increasingly rapid swings up and down in public confidence . . . has weakened, consequently, the president's staying power in office and his ability to govern.

Yet it cannot be denied that there is something characteristically American about the individualistic-marketplace model. Such mediating political institutions as the political parties have never been especially popular in America. The absence of long-run governmental popularity and power does not go totally against the American grain. And the "people" have always longed for the sense, however illusionary, of a direct relationship with politicians that modern technological innovations now provide. *Therefore, if the parties are to regain their preeminent role in the nominating process, they must aggressively pursue strategies to take their case to the mass media marketplace and convince political consumers of the benefits of institutional mediation and stable governmental leadership.*

The need for the parties to fight for their survival in the mass media marketplace exposes the most serious shortcomings in the party countercultural alternative envisioned by New Liberal intellectuals. For the idea of a Jeffersonian "ward system" existing independently from the mainstream mass media culture appears to be a particularly unrealistic process for nominating presidential candidates in the latter part of the twentieth century. The New Liberal alternative, as Michael Walzer acknowledged in *The New Republic*, does seem "to express a certain hankering for an older form of democracy, inappropriate to a mass society and insufficiently accessible to the mass media." *Nevertheless, stripped of its "countercultural" illusions, the New Liberal model does emphasize the truth that the political parties and their presidential candidates must represent some identifiable community of political interests in order to survive as major institutional entities.* As James David Barber has written, those figures "who urge the revival of parties as abstract good things in themselves or look to the reinvigoration of the jumbo coalitions of years gone by are marching up a blind alley. Purpose comes first, then party."

The often cited danger in emphasizing "the purpose" of parties has been that they would split into numerous ideological factions. In the future, however, this risk may have to be partially assumed if the nomination struggle for the party label is going to stand for anything in the minds of the voters. Yet the eventual task of appealing to a majority of the consumers should continue to prove a powerful force in moderating the ideological nature of the package that the parties eventually place in the political marketplace. *Moreover, the use of a caucus nominating system that opens itself up to mass media coverage might be able to promote at least a measure of the public spirit and civic identity that the New Liberals rightly see as the great cohesive force in any party system.* In at least those states with a still relatively strong party organization, this kind of "mass media" caucus system might prove to be an attractive alternative to the use of primaries. And if the Iowa experience in the 1980 nomination campaign is a good example, intensive media coverage could also greatly increase the general rates of public participation and diminish the rather elitist cast of the countercultural caucus model.

The fact that the parties must build themselves from the ground up argues against the governmental nationalization proposals in the party protectionist model of New Conservative intellectuals. In all likelihood the role of the national parties in the nominating process cannot be indefinitely prolonged by legislative fiat. Like all other "protectionist" proposals, the New Conservative model fails to give due credit to the dynamism of competition and change that constitutes the lifeblood of all healthy institutional systems. Far from contributing to the vitality of the two-party system, the party protectionist model could easily contribute to its eventual decay. Professor Ladd himself has acknowledged the danger of "excessive governmental regulation of the parties."

However, even if "nationalizing" the nominating process of the two-party system represents too radical a departure with many possible unintended consequences, the general New Conservative goal of promoting a mix of proposals to fortify the party system against the disintegrating trends of the political marketplace is obviously essential. It is true, as Professor Ladd has pointed out, that the state as well as federal governments have been involved in various aspects of the party nominating process dating back to the Progressive era. The federal government has become especially involved in the area of campaign finance. *Thus it would be a logical step to encourage congressional legislation subsidizing the cost of television time for both major parties during the nomination and general election campaign—especially if the legislation includes provisions for minor party access on some equitable basis.* Changes in campaign finance legislation would not have to stop with the funding of television time. *A more far-reaching proposal deserving consideration is that federal funding of major party presidential candidates during the nomination campaign be rechanneled to the party national committees. The party committees would then become responsible for the distribution of campaign funds.*

Finally, the parties can be encouraged to allow major and elected public officials to comprise a significant minority bloc of uncommitted delegates at the national convention. It is misleading, however, to advertise this proposal as a way to restore a role for "the bosses" at the national convention. For the inclusion of such delegates in this plebiscitary age can only be justified by the fact that all of these officials have stood for election and are thus accountable to broad cross sections of the party or general public.

We do not mean to suggest that these recommendations represent a complete set of proposals or the only feasible ways to synthesize the opposing intellectual models for the presidential nominating process. Perhaps advocates of each different position will object that such attempted syntheses succeed only in emasculating the force of the respective visions. Especially in the current polarized intellectual atmosphere, the mere hope for reconciliation and synthesis might be dismissed as chimerical. But we continue to believe that American politics and intellectual thought operate best when they reflect a sense of what Richard Hofstadter once called "comity"—the ability to respect and benefit from the legitimate but opposing insights of contending interests and viewpoints.

Index

About The American Assembly

The American Assembly was established by Dwight D. Eisenhower at Columbia University in 1950. It holds nonpartisan meetings and publishes authoritative books to illuminate issues of United States policy.

An affiliate of Columbia, with offices in the Graduate School of Business, the Assembly is a national educational institution incorporated in the State of New York.

The Assembly seeks to provide information, stimulate discussion, and evoke independent conclusions in matters of vital public interest.

AMERICAN ASSEMBLY SESSIONS

At least two national programs are initiated each year. Authorities are retained to write background papers presenting essential data and defining the main issues in each subject.

A group of men and women representing a broad range of experience, competence, and American leadership meet for several days to discuss the Assembly topic and consider alternatives for national policy.

All Assemblies follow the same procedure. The background papers are sent to participants in advance of the Assembly. The Assembly meets in small groups for four or five lengthy periods. All groups use the same agenda. At the close of these informal sessions, participants adopt in plenary session a final report of findings and recommendations.

Regional, state, and local Assemblies are held following the national session at Arden House. Assemblies have also been held in England, Switzerland, Malaysia, Canada, the Caribbean, South America, Central America, the Philippines, and Japan. Over one hundred thirty institutions have cosponsored one or more Assemblies.

ARDEN HOUSE

Home of The American Assembly and scene of the national sessions is Arden House which was given to Columbia University in 1950 by W. Averell Harriman. E. Roland Harriman joined his brother in contributing toward adaptation of the property for conference purposes. The buildings and surrounding land, known as the Harriman Campus of Columbia University, are 50 miles north of New York City.

Arden House is a distinguished conference center. It is self-supporting and operates throughout the year for use by organizations with educational objectives.

AMERICAN ASSEMBLY BOOKS

The background papers for each Assembly are published in cloth and paperbound editions for use by individuals, libraries, businesses, public agencies, nongovernmental organizations, educational institutions, discussion and service groups. In this way the deliberations of Assembly sessions are continued and extended.

The subjects of Assembly programs to date are:

1951——United States-Western Europe Relationships
1952——Inflation
1953——Economic Security for Americans
1954——The United States' Stake in the United Nations
——The Federal Government Service
1955——United States Agriculture
——The Forty-Eight States
1956——The Representation of the United States Abroad
——The United States and the Far East
1957——International Stability and Progress
——Atoms for Power
1958——The United States and Africa
——United States Monetary Policy
1959——Wages, Prices, Profits, and Productivity
——The United States and Latin America
1960——The Federal Government and Higher Education
——The Secretary of State
——Goals for Americans
1961——Arms Control: Issues for the Public
——Outer Space: Prospects for Man and Society
1962——Automation and Technological Change
——Cultural Affairs and Foreign Relations
1963——The Population Dilemma
——The United States and the Middle East
1964——The United States and Canada
——The Congress and America's Future
1965——The Courts, the Public, and the Law Explosion

1965—The United States and Japan
1966—State Legislatures in American Politics
     —A World of Nuclear Powers?
     —The United States and the Philippines
     —Challenges to Collective Bargaining
1967—The United States and Eastern Europe
     —Ombudsmen for American Government?
1968—Uses of the Seas
     —Law in a Changing America
     —Overcoming World Hunger
1969—Black Economic Development
     —The States and the Urban Crisis
1970—The Health of Americans
     —The United States and the Caribbean
1971—The Future of American Transportation
     —Public Workers and Public Unions
1972—The Future of Foundations
     —Prisoners in America
1973—The Worker and the Job
     —Choosing the President
1974—The Good Earth of America
     —On Understanding Art Museums
     —Global Companies
1975—Law and the American Future
     —Women and the American Economy
1976—Nuclear Power Controversy
     —Jobs for Americans
     —Capital for Productivity and Jobs
1977—The Ethics of Corporate Conduct
     —The Performing Arts and American Society
1978—Running the American Corporation
     —Race for the Presidency
1979—Energy Conservation and Public Policy
     —Disorders in Higher Education
     —Youth Employment and Public Policy
1980—The Economy and the President
     —The Farm and the City
     —Mexico and the United States
1981—The China Factor
     —Military Service in the United States
     —Ethnic Relations in America
1982—The Future of American Political Parties

1982——The American Economy in Transition
1983——The Future of American Financial Service Institutions

Second Editions, Revised:

1962——The United States and the Far East
1963——The United States and Latin America
    ——The United States and Africa
1964——United States Monetary Policy
1965——The Federal Government Service
    ——The Representation of the United States Abroad
1968——Cultural Affairs and Foreign Relations
    ——Outer Space: Prospects for Man and Society
1969——The Population Dilemma
1973——The Congress and America's Future
1975——The United States and Japan